"While providing a co~~i~~ the historical develop~~i~~ offers a winsome and Christian college and C ~~......~~ ~~...~~......... I know that board members, administrators, faculty members, parents, and students will all find this important proposal to be quite helpful. I am happy to recommend *Learning to Love.*"

David S. Dockery, PhD, President, International Alliance for Christian Education

"Alex Sosler is a pastoral guide for students entering their college years with trepidation and uncertainty. In this accessible and winsome book, he orients students to a college experience that will set them on a life-long pilgrimage toward rightly ordered loves and embodied wisdom."

Jeffrey Bilbro, PhD, Associate Professor of English, Grove City College and Editor-in-Chief at *Front Porch Republic.* co-author (with Jack Baker) of *Wendell Berry and Higher Education: Cultivating Virtues of Place*

"So many of the best books on Christian learning were written long ago, but we need living authors to gloss those texts to make their meaning clear for us now. Alex Sosler's *Learning to Love* reminds us of the journey that is education: life-long, full of joy, love, and other people. If you're entering college or you know someone who is, this book should act as an invitation to the pilgrimage that is Christian education."

Jessica Hooten Wilson, PhD, Seaver College Scholar of Liberal Arts at Pepperdine University

"Alex Sosler offers a much-needed corrective to the most prevalent misconceptions about higher ed in our time. In prose that is conversational and engaging, he invites us into an education that rejects both Gnostic hyper-rationalism and reductive materialism, offering instead an Augustinian vision of education as the ordering and expanding of proper love. Sosler advocates for an educational pilgrimage that leads to the embodied and whole-hearted pursuit of wisdom and of wonder. This is a book that should be read by every college freshman and by every parent with a child considering college."

Benjamin Myers, PhD, Professor of English and Literature, Director of the Honors College, Oklahoma Baptist University

"Many of today's college students are not sure why they're in college or what their end goal should be (apart from gainful employment, important as that is). Alex Sosler steps into this confusion and offers a compelling vision for Christian college education. With a keen awareness of the culture and a smart but relatable voice, Alex invites students to move from transaction to transformation as they put love for God and neighbor at the center of learning. This is a book I wish I had when I started my journey at a Christian liberal arts college decades ago, and—as someone who is passionate about preparing young people for a life of thriving after college—it's one I'm eager to share!"

Erica Young Reitz, MA, author of *After College* and founder of After College Transition

"For people launching into college, and from college into the world, here is an intriguing guide to consider what that education is about, and to embrace it responsibly. Appropriately central is the theme: we love in order to know. The goal of college is to cultivate lovers—lovers of the real."

Esther Lightcap Meek, PhD, Author of *Longing to Know: The Philosophy of Knowledge for Ordinary People*, *Loving to Know: Introducing Covenant Epistemology*, and *A Little Manual for Knowing*

"*Learning to Love* lifts our eyes to the vision of a flourishing life. Tethered closely to an Augustinian approach, it is good only because of rightly ordered loves and an identity that is ultimately found in Christ. The book outlines the path of beauty, truth, and goodness in which Dr. Sosler offers a compelling vision for a liberal arts education.

In a very straightforward, insightful, well-researched, and avant-garde manner. *Learning to Love* is a traveling companion for the student seeking substance and depth on their collegiate journey. It is a journey worth packing for, but more importantly worth reading about."

Matt Koons, PhD, Headmaster, Cuyahoga Valley Christian Academy

"I am grateful for a new text which addresses the perennial question, 'What is college for?' While accounting for contemporary reductionistic trends within the academy, Sosler promotes an expansive and holistic vision of higher education derived from historic Christian praxis. Faculty and students alike will benefit from *Learning to Love*, as the book critiques insufficient models of education, while reorienting readers towards a pedagogy rooted in love. Sosler's love for higher education is evident, which makes his prose all the more compelling."

Jeffrey Tabone, PhD, Assistant Professor of Honors Humanities and Director of Programs and Student Formation for the John Wesley Honors College of Indiana Wesleyan University

"In *Learning to Love*, Alex Sosler offers a winsome and cogent answer to the complex and fraught question, 'What is college for?' He casts a vibrant vision for not only the college experience, but a lifelong pilgrimage of learning."

Drew Moser, PhD, Professor of Higher Education, Taylor University and author of *The Enneagram of Discernment*

"Sosler offers a probing and accessible diagnosis of what ails modern higher education. Even if one disagrees with his proposed treatment for the ailment, the reader will find a wealth of resources to inquire into the purpose of education, and the ineradicable (but often suppressed) desire to live a life worth living."

David Henreckson, PhD, Director of Weyerhauser Center for Christian Faith and Learning at Whitworth University

"*Learning to Love* brings the Christian concern for Christ-centeredness in all things into a conversation with the humanist ideals of liberal education, in order to enrich both. Dispensing with the utilitarian priorities of many secular schools today, Professor Sosler approaches learning through the Augustinian lens of rightly-ordered loves, operating under the guidance of divine grace. Many students and parents will find this a valuable aid to grasp the underlying principles of higher education, and use those principles to find just the right college for mind and soul alike."

Jeremy Wayne Tate, MA, President of Classical Learning Test

LEARNING TO LOVE

LEARNING TO LOVE

CHRISTIAN HIGHER EDUCATION
AS PILGRIMAGE

Dr. Alex Sosler

Alex Sosler

FALLS CITY PRESS
Beaver Falls, Pennsylvania
www.fallscitypress.com

LEARNING TO LOVE: CHRISTIAN HIGHER EDUCATION AS PILGRIMAGE

©2023 Falls City Press by Alex Sosler

2108 Seventh Avenue
Beaver Falls, PA 15010
www.fallscitypress.com

Cover Design by Kristin Slebodnik

Library of Congress Cataloging-in-Publication Data

Sosler, Alex, 1989—

    p. cm.
Includes bibliographical references.

Identifiers:
ISBN: 978-1-7369184-8-7 (print)

1. Christian college students—Religious life. 1. Title.
BV4531.3.S89 2023 (print)

Printed in the United States of America

Contents

To Mom and Dad,
Who loved me into life
And were my first teachers.

FOREWORD

I went to college many years ago. We had no cell phones and no computers. Instead, we took turns on what was called a pay phone in the hallway of our residence hall, and we completed papers on what was called a typewriter. Here is something else that was different: all four years of my college education at a private institution cost less than $10K. That's not per year; that's total.

These and other facts of times gone by doesn't mean that my college experience was altogether different than yours is today. There were classes and books and tests of course, as well as social events, sporting venues, and local opportunities. There were also friendships (including some that flourish to this day), flings, fun, skipped classes, and too much time in the dining hall. And, especially early on, there was a tangible sense that a new chapter of my life was unfolding.

In retrospect, however, I assure you that my college years were formative. In the context of this book that you now hold in your hands, college was instrumental in helping me to "order my loves" or to develop "a direction for my pilgrimage." Or, in the context of a book that I read many years after college entitled *The Fabric of Faithfulness*, college was the place that I was introduced to and subsequently embraced a vision of life for all of life rooted in Christian faith. Further, during college I observed this totalizing vision being fleshed out in authentic ways in the lives of colleagues around me (both faculty and friends), and that continued to be reinforced in the years post-college with both continuing and new friends and co-workers.

At least two clarifications are in order. First, I don't want to suggest that college turned the lights on for me—all of a sudden and brightly to boot—and that I have basked in the glow since then. I mean, it wasn't that there weren't moments in which I felt as though I experienced an "aha." But I came to realize that faith and life formation is more of an unfolding experience that takes time and tending and comrades. It also always unfolds (and even strains) in the context of other loves that compete for your affections. For example, Alex gives you three examples of other loves that may misdirect you in your Christian college journey, all of which are rooted in a misplaced reliance on oneself rather than on the Lord of the universe.

Second, and relatedly, faith and life formation continue across one's lifespan. While it may be true that college provided an opportunity for me that made (more) sense of previous life experiences, laid a more robust and compelling framework for faith-shaped learning and living, and offered experiences and persons that were excellent guides for the journey, my formative experience in college wasn't meant to end when I got a diploma. Rather, it became a launching point for new journeys since graduation. I would like to think that my formation not only continues, but has also become more deeply ingrained, more wise, more nuanced…more! You would be spot on to recognize this as part and parcel of maturing in Christ (cf., Col. 1:28-29), of making and solidifying commitments over time, and of having one's devotion to Jesus become more second nature in all that one does.

I don't want to keep you much longer from diving enthusiastically into this book, but I do want to mention three more things briefly. Each has something to do with this book, but in relationship to my own experience as a Christian educator over the years. First, this book is written as if it is in a conversation with you. That is, Professor Sosler's writing style is akin to talking with you over a cup of coffee. Cultivating humanity in all that we do—including writing a book—strikes me as precisely the kind of thing that God has had in mind from the beginning (i.e., making a way for us to be most fully human in allegiance to God and His kingdom) is precisely what makes a college education most powerful; and, is precisely what commends itself to us as the way to live our lives daily. Even keeping the chapters on the short side in terms of length reflects a certain embrace of a more human communication effort and may even promote additional dialog beyond the class period. That resonates with me as an appropriate and important byproduct of Christian higher education.

Second, I lament that sometimes some (maybe many) students aren't engaged in their college education because it seems so different than their lived lives. They sense a disconnect about what goes on in classrooms and what goes on in life. My sense is that Christian higher education should not be this way. If Christianity concerns "life and life abundant" and if classrooms are places in which various areas of life are explored, then students should readily and enthusiastically see relationships between class and life. I hope that you will find that this book strives to bolster these connections by using a variety of sources that range from athletics to music to movies to personal experiences…and to scholarly sources.

Finally, I have spent my career thinking about Christian higher education. Plenty of Christian colleges exist, plenty of students attend them, and plenty of things have been written about them over many years. I hope that readers of this book will listen closely, particularly to Chapter 7 to the end because, in them, Dr. Sosler identifies a "reorienting" to what he hopes students will come to make of their Christian collegiate learning experience: gift, charity, belonging, practice, community, and commitment. What a list! The extent to which our journeys are formed by these things—both during college and for the years that the Lord gives us beyond college—will make all the difference in living faithfully and in bringing honor to the one who, even now, sits on the throne.

David Guthrie, PhD

Author of *Dreaming Dreams for Christian Higher Education*

Welcome to the Christian College

"The university is not only, and maybe not even primarily
about knowledge. It is . . . after our imagination, our
heart, our desire. It wants to make us into certain kinds
of people who desire a certain telos, who are primed to
pursue a vision of the good life."

James KA Smith, *Desiring the Kingdom*

"Sometimes it takes a long time to learn how to play like yourself."

Miles Davis

Welcome to college, fellow pilgrim. This journey can change
your life—whether it be 2 years or 4 years or 6 years.[1] However long it takes, you will be a different person at the end of
your time. The goal of this book is to align who you want to
be with the choices you make over the next several years. In
other words, based on your destination, you need a roadmap
on how to approach the trail and how to get there.

I remember heading to college for the first time. I was excited. Surrounded by peers, away from my parents' rule and guidance, I was beginning the journey to adulthood. There were mainly two things I wanted from college: to play a sport (soccer in my case) and to get a degree (which would allow me to get a "good" job). I'm a simple man. The goals I had and the destination at which I desired to arrive dictated the way I traveled the road.

I know many of you come to college at different stages of life. Perhaps you took a gap year or were in the military or started a career first. But I'm guessing most of you came to college as "the plan," or at least "a plan." As you read this, you're likely in your teens. Whether you like it or not, most of society views you as a youth. But by the end of your time in college, people will expect you to be a young adult—with all the responsibilities that being an adult requires.

One of your tasks over the next four years is to mature into a capable and competent human. Historically, helping students mature has been one of college's primary purposes: developing young people to think, act, and love in more mature ways. But the truth is that you won't end up as a mature, whole adult by osmosis. You don't wake up on the day of your graduation and find out you are suddenly fully formed. That would be like assuming if I thought a lot about basketball and spent time around people who played basketball, then I would be a good basketball player. Well, unfortunately, it doesn't quite work that way. It takes intention, discipline, and *work*. You have to learn who you want to be and practice being that person. College exists to help you form your sense of identity, purpose, and meaning. Your role is to find and pursue the most compelling vision for your life.

To chart the course ahead for the next four years, we need to have some sense of where we are going. Like a pilgrim, at times in college you will feel like you are wandering aimlessly. Why did you come here again? Why did you pick *this* school? Shouldn't you be making money rather than going into debt? These are typical questions. This little book is designed to be a guide for you on your journey—both for when you see the destination clearly and for times when you don't know where you are going.

Ideally, this book will be used as you begin (or continue) your college career. Even if you have never articulated the goal of your life, you are pursuing some dream. You have some vision of a life worth living. You are not a wandering traveler. You're going somewhere. You are a pilgrim with a destination. By the end of this book, the goal is to have a clearer sense of the purpose of the college years. All things may not be clear by the end of your college career (spoiler alert: they won't). But the role of this book is to encourage a sense of direction for these years. Based on what college is for (its purpose and mission), how can you live into what you were made for (your purpose and mission)? The college years can help you discover a vision of the good life and expand your understanding of what the good life is. But how do you get from here to there? Over the course of this book, I'll attempt to develop a map for your pilgrimage.

A Foundational Journey

> "We seem to be born homesick, and that homesickness is meant to lead us into a life of pilgrimage."
>
> Walker Percy

The pilgrim motif has long been a paradigm for the Christian life. The writer of Hebrews describes the faithful of the past as strangers and exiles on earth seeking a home which they never experienced in their earthly life (Heb. 11:13). Even as Peter describes Christians as a holy priesthood and a chosen race, a few verses later he calls the church sojourners and exiles (1 Pet. 9, 11): travelers without a home. The fourth-century African St. Augustine picks up this theme as he describes our hearts as on a continual journey for rest or home. Dante, an Italian poet of the thirteenth century, penned a winding tale about the journey to God through three books titled *The Divine Comedy*. Within it, the soul is personified as it travels through different levels of the afterlife: through hell (*Inferno*), through purgatory (*Purgatorio*), and eventually to paradise (*Paradiso*). In paradise, the soul finally finds its ultimate rest as it rests in God. The hobbits in Tolkien's *The Lord of the Rings* do not like adventure and would rather stay at home, but central to the story of *The Lord of the Rings* are hobbits who leave the Shire to accomplish a mission at the top of Mount Doom. Today, many religious traditions celebrate holy pilgrimages to certain cities or along certain paths seeking spiritual renewal and inspiration. Like Walker Percy mentions, there's a homesickness that leads us on a pilgrimage.

In 1678, John Bunyan wrote a book called *Pilgrim's Progress*. The book became a classic, and you may have read it growing up. Bunyan was a lowly tinker in England's prestigious culture. He was not educated. He was not ordained. He fixed trinkets around the house and earned a meager income. He did not have status. But he was also a preacher, which angered the powers that be. He was put in prison for holding a church service that was not approved by the official church. And in prison, this lowly, uneducated preacher wrote a book that we still read nearly 400 years later.

The book is an allegory of the Christian life. He compares this life to a pilgrimage. A man named "Christian" is the main character. (Clever, huh?) He passes through different cities and different temptations. The Christian journey is not a one-size-fits-all trek. At different times–at different stages–we're all exposed to different realities. What someone struggles with when they're young may be something someone else wrestles with later on in life. What's hard as a young adult is different on your deathbed. However, we all pass through certain hardships with certain vulnerabilities on the pilgrimage of life, and Bunyan illustrates these realities through story.[2]

In *Learning to Love*, I take this paradigm of pilgrimage and apply it to certain realities in college. Each stage of college life has enticements and attractions that may lure you off the path. To accomplish this, I'll need to do some deconstruction before I set a proper foundation for the pilgrimage. My goal is for you to re-image what education is—from a dry, stuffy, and dull task to a joyful, life-giving, wonderful journey.

To be fair, the journey I lead you on doesn't isn't a comprehensive map for college. For example, the temptation of hedonistic pleasure may seem all-consuming at times. You want to have "fun" and "party" in college—which may mean some mix of alcoholic beverages and pursuit of a love interest. You may play a sport, but I'm not going to talk much about the "City of Athletics" and the certain vulnerabilities you'll face there—whether that be viewing your worth in playing time or the difficulties of balancing school and practice. These are real struggles—but the purpose of this book is to deal with your intellectual journey—and through your intellectual journey, your life's pilgrimage.

Introducing Fellow Pilgrims

I want to tell you about four different students. These students are created from my combined interactions with students over the years, so their names and details are manufactured, but their tendencies are real.

The first person is named Jonathan. He shows up to my New Testament Survey class ready to learn. He's eager and excited about the Bible. Having been raised in a Christian home, he's here at a Christian college to deepen his faith. The Bible is all he wants to know, and he views his general education classes—literature, mathematics, history—as an impediment to taking the classes that are most important: Bible classes. He struggles in any other class because he's just not interested in what they have to offer. He's here at college for "Christian knowledge," which for him is a very limited sort of knowledge.

Isabel is another student. She's earned straight A's ever since she can remember. She's disciplined, engaged, and passionate about studying. She may have been called a know-it-all or teacher's pet from time-to-time, because she always knows the right answer, always does what's right, and offers a lot of corrections. ("Well, actually....") She is great at memorization and recitation. She's at college to show off and to grow in knowledge. And of course, she wants the best grades. While her friends are out at parties, you can find Isabel studying for her next exam or completing homework early.

Let's call the third character Peyton. She has been trained to ask the one question that people ask in college: "What are you going to do with that degree?" And so, she's practical. She majors in a degree that makes sense, which means it makes money. She doesn't care so much about learning if it doesn't have any practical use. She's at college to get a good job. She charts her life according to upward mobility and financial status. The good life is the wealthy life.

Lastly, there's Isaiah. Isaiah lives up to his prophetic name. He's always had a strong sense of right and wrong, of seeing the lowly and downcast. Isaiah sees the world with an eye toward justice: of lifting the poor and bringing down the proud.

He often wonders why he's in college classes when there is so much pain and suffering in the world. He should be out there in the real world being an advocate. He's at college to make a difference through social activism.

I wonder which student you relate to most. Maybe there are a few characteristics of the students that you are drawn to. To be sure, each student is after a good thing. Biblical wisdom, learning, a job, and activism are all good things. However, every good thing, when given supreme importance, results in disorder. What a student loves most has great control over the life they pursue. Because here's what every college shapes: what you love most.

Finding the Path

Part of our task as pilgrims in the college voyage is to know the past. To know where you are going, you must know where you have been. I do not know your upbringing or school experience, but you have been formed to imagine education a certain way. As sure as you have a sense of the good life and the things you love the most, you also have a sense of what education is. Maybe education is the necessary chore you must do in order to achieve what you really want. Maybe education is about listening passively at a desk as the teacher dumps information into your brain receptacle, and your job is to memorize what the teacher said so you can recite back what they said to you at a later date. That's called a test—and it supposedly shows you how smart you are. Or perhaps school is just the thing you did during the day over the past 12 years.

Part I of this book provides a brief history of the university to give you a sense of where you are now. Considering the way college has developed over the years, how has it impacted the way we think about education? What are some things you currently imagine that need re-imagining? How does that affect your pilgrimage? After shedding some light on our path in Chapter 1, Chapter 2 explores the rich heritage of education in the Christian liberal arts tradition. This chapter lays a foundation as it seeks to answer: "What is a Christian liberal arts school?" Chapter 3—"The College for Thinkers"—explains the rise of "natural" explanations due to the elevation of the mind. Colleges lost their religious foundation and were more concerned with creating new knowledge rather than the moral formation of students. In Chapter 4, "The College for Workers," we investigate the university's move to the practical. In this model, college tends to be mostly for job training. It's all about finding your own personal, unique job. You are valuable as long as you contribute to the economy (i.e., make money and spend money). In the final shift of the university described in Chapter 5—"The College for Critics"—we look at the paradigm we are beginning to see in the university. In this view, knowledge is about power, and the intellectuals who went before us were just seeking dominance. Statements that claimed to be the truth are inherently oppressive. Therefore, we ought to question and tear down the heritage that came before us. It's no good. Instead, college is about finding your own personal truth. There is no truth that exists beyond what you feel and believe.

In each of these chapters, I'll describe different ways of understanding college as certain "cities"—like we're pilgrims making our way on the journey. Your particular persuasions for a city's ultimate love may pull you in certain directions. But each model city puts you on a certain trajectory for life. A certain love defined in a city causes you to view the purpose of education, and the purpose of your life, in a definitive way. The danger is that we could think of any of the cities as our main destination. While these cities are attractive in many ways, I will attempt to show them as seductive reductions of what the best education can be. To be fair, it's not that these cities are bad as much as they are limited. I like to describe these cities like St. Augustine described Egypt.[3] Augustine describes education like Israel leaving Egypt in the Exodus. God commands the Israelites that before they leave, they should take the Egyptians' gold and riches. In a similar way, the task of faithful Christian learning requires that we plunder the riches of the Egyptians—and I'll argue for the riches of each of these cities that we pass through. But Egypt is not the destination; Mount Zion is. So, if we remain in the metaphysical Egypt, then we will have a false vision of the good life. A Christian education gives us the vision and skills and loves to get to the proper destination.

We'll track these movements in higher education and see how we've all been led astray in our understanding of and approach to education. We need to clear away some of the brush before we can see the path that lay ahead. Chapter 6 provides a holistic approach to education—a rightly ordered education includes the classics, intellectual development, and vocational preparation and discernment. But education is ultimately about what you love.

With the destination in sight and the path clear, I'll suggest a few ways we ought to view and pursue an education in the second half of the book. With love as central to the educational task, love animates how we go about learning. If love animates us, then we can see new discoveries as gifts that we receive more than knowledge that we attain (Chapter 7). Chapter 8 describes the posture or habits through which we learn, namely, by charity. The motivation for learning is a communal belonging as shown in Chapter 9, and we need good practices in our pursuit of not merely knowledge but greater wisdom (Chapter 10). Community is the theme of the final chapter as all our educational pursuits are not individual affairs. Mentors and friends

can assist our educational journeys as each of us also have a
valuable role to play in campus life.

Conclusion

My goal in this book is not to tell you the right things to
learn, but to re-envision what learning is and what it entails. In essence, I want you to cast your vision higher. In
the words of my friend, David Guthrie, I want you to dream
bigger and better dreams in higher education. My desire is
for you to understand that more is at stake than a future job
or letter grades. In the pages that follow, I want to dream
together about the person you want to become, and how
education can help you pursue a life worth living.

Come on the journey with me!

Discussion Questions

1. What are your hopes and dreams as you enter college?
    What do you hope happens here?
2. What are some of your fears about college?
3. How do you plan to go about your college years pur-
    suing your hopes and managing your fears?
4. If you were to describe a photograph taken on your
    graduation day, what would the picture look like?
    How would you describe yourself? Who and what is
    in the photo?
5. As you think of your time in college, describe the
    person you hope to become.

Notes

1. To quote Chris Farley in *Tommy Boy:* "You know a lot of people go to college for seven years." David Spade in response, "I know. And they're called doctors."

2. I'm not telling you what to do, but it's a book you should read before you graduate if you haven't already.

3. See Augustine, *On Christian Teaching* (New York: Oxford University Press, 2008), II, 40.

CHAPTER 1

The Pilgrim's Path

"This hill, though high, I covet to ascend;

The difficulty will not me offend.
For I perceive the way to life lies here.
Come, pluck up, heart; let's neither faint nor fear.
Better, though difficult, the right way to go,
Than wrong, though easy, where the end is woe."

John Bunyan, *Pilgrim's Progress*

Have you ever hiked in the dark?

I teach at Montreat College. Montreat is a shortened form of "mountain retreat." Predictably, our campus is in the mountains. And if you're wondering, it's wonderful. Even ugly days of rain or gray are pretty days. One of the benefits of such a campus is that there are wonderful trails to hike. From my office door, I can take a half-mile walk and be on a trail system that travels hundreds of miles full of beautiful views, serene nature, and quiet. (With a house full of three young kids, quiet is a nice reprieve in my life). You may not have kids, but in a busy campus with full residence halls, sometimes it's nice to get away and alone.

The mountain "cove" of our campus is surrounded by seven mountain peaks known as the "Seven Sisters." There's a 14-mile hiking trail along the ridge to hit each of the "sisters" in one hike. A few of my friends and I attempted the journey a few years ago. We started in the dark of the pre-dawn morning.

I do not know if you know this, but the thing about the dark is that you can't see. And the thing about where we started is that it was steep—at times, crawling-on-your-hands-and-knees steep. Not to mention I had recently seen a bobcat gnawing on a dead possum in my front yard and bears are an ever-present reality in the Carolina mountains. I couldn't see threats or dangers unless they were too close for comfort. And I like comfort.

Sure, we had headlamps and flashlights to guide our way, but I was relieved as the sun peaked over the mountain tops. The dark sky began to turn a deep shade of blue. Then light blue. Then pink, as the sun hit the clouds. All of a sudden, I could see. The beauty of the mountains was always there. I just couldn't see it before. The mountains did not change. I did. The beauty became visible as the light shined in the darkness.

As you start your collegiate pilgrimage, you may feel like you are in the dark. Your darkness could be due to the fact that you've never thought about education for yourself. Or it could be because you've listened to what you've been told about the purpose of college. Either way, one of the goals of college is to contemplate your life and the world. If we never deeply consider or learn from the past, then we will be tossed and turned by the waves of current events and whatever is the

newest trend on TikTok. To be a substantive person, a person
of depth, we need some wisdom and light.

This task of finding wisdom will be hard. It's easy to not
reflect, to go with the flow, to listen to the latest fad, and to
do what seems popular at the moment. But the worthwhile
way may be the hard way. Sometimes, better to take the
hard path and end up where you desire than the easy way
that leads to despair. As Robert Frost poetically penned,
"Two roads diverged in a wood, and I—I took the one less
traveled by, And that has made all the difference."[1] Oftentimes, the hard way, the way not traveled, ends up making
the best difference. Wouldn't it be better if we had some
convictions to direct our life, so we are not just responding
to the world but taking some responsibility for the world
we help create?

Before we continue, I want to shed some light on the path
by reimagining who you are and what education is about.
This first chapter is like a flashlight. It can orientate us a bit to
the trail before the sun comes. The goal is to move from the
flashlight in the dark to the brightness of the shining sun. In
the light of the sun, we can better walk the path of education.

Who Are You?

What would you say if I asked, "Who are you?" Maybe you'd
answer with a series of descriptions: male or female, where
you're from, what you like to do, your family of origin, etc.
Or you may tell me what other people have told you: You're
a woman. You're an athlete. You're a future employee. You're
an honors student. Often, we absorb the names others call us,
and sometimes those names are limiting.

How can we recover a true sense of self? How can we
discover who we are in a way that isn't merely self-expression
or what others tell us? How can others help us self-reflect and

discover? These are questions of identity. In today's world, it is often difficult to discover or discern your identity.

One of the ways we discern who we really are is by trying on ideas and seeing how they fit. In many ways, experiencing new ideas is what a college education is for: reading, writing, listening, and responding to ideas to see if they "fit" you. As we see and understand how humans expressed themselves, we better understand our particular humanity in the present. Learning to ask and see, "What does it mean to be human?" or "What do we have in common across ages?" we come to understand our own identity. When I read a novel by Flannery O'Connor or a speech by Martin Luther King, Jr., they are expressing themselves, sure. But they are expressing themselves in a way that makes better sense of myself. An O'Connor short story can help me realize that humanity is not "good country people" but deeply flawed or self-righteous people—even myself. A speech by Martin Luther King, Jr. can convict me in the ways that I'm lazy for injustice because a situation seems like it does not affect me. Both offer opportunities of formation that may be difficult for me to discern on my own.

Every education assumes something about human personhood. In a book of essays entitled *What Are We Doing Here?* (which is a good question to ask as you get started in your college career), Marilynne Robinson wrote, "How we think about ourselves has everything to do with how we act toward one another."[2] Are we all just data-processing systems like complex computers? That will affect how you think about learning in the classroom. Are we merely future employees who need to be trained for job skills? Then we will always value only what is practical. How we think about ourselves will affect how we treat one another. Who are you? This is one of the most important questions with which we engage life and learning.

In this book, I'm going to use the words "soul" or "heart" because I think at our fundamental level, that's what distinguishes us from other creatures and dignifies humanity. In using these terms, I do not mean to suggest a dichotomy between body/soul or material/immaterial as if we could be disconnected from the world or our bodies. However, I think we can all recognize some essential, non-physical part of us. There is an aspect of you that is not just a piece of meat or brain chemicals. You have an eternal soul of infinite worth that makes you unique and dignified. You don't have to believe in God to believe in the soul. On this "inner person," pastor Tim Keller writes, "Our heart is the center of our personality, the seat of our fundamental commitments, the control center of the whole person. What is in the heart determines what we think, do, and feel—since mind, will, and emotions are all rooted there."[3] The heart is the central aspect of our humanity, as Pabbie says in *Frozen*, "The heart is not so easily changed but the head can be persuaded." When Anna gets her head frozen, it can change, but when Elsa freezes her heart, that's when the real danger starts. The heart is the center of commitments and loves, and we live from our commitments and loves.

If we can see each other as souls, then that changes everything about education. Marilynne Robinson is a novelist. In a book called *Jack*, the main character could be described as a "prodigal." He was raised in a minister's family and taught right from wrong, but he never quite fit in. So, he ran away from home to the dismay of his family and community. In the novel, he is half-homeless and can't figure his life out even though his family tries to help. As the story unfolds, Jack meets a girl named Della. And here's what Della says about this "bum," Jack:

> Once in a lifetime you look at a stranger and you see
> a soul, a glorious presence out of place in the world.
> And if you love God, every choice is made for you.
> There is no turning away. You've seen the mystery—
> you've seen what life is about. What it's for. And a soul
> has no earthly qualities, no history among the things of
> this world, no guilt or injury or failure. No more than
> a flame would have. There is nothing to be said about it
> except that it is a holy human soul. And it is a miracle
> when you recognize it.[4]

She saw the mystery. That's what I mean when I say "soul."
Each individual you meet in the classroom is an eternal
soul. Their worth does not depend on how smart they are,
their skin color, their economic status, or any other aspect.
Their existence—your existence—is a miracle. It changes
everything about how you view yourself and how you treat
others. Existing as a soul is central to one's identity.

Why Are You Here?

Here's what I think college is for: ordering and expanding
our loves, and therefore our lives. You likely have some preconceived notions about what love is. Throughout the book,
I try to redefine our contemporary notions of love. For now,
when I say I love, I mean Jesus in the Great Commandment
type of love, that we should love God with all our mind,
strength, and soul, and love our neighbors as ourselves. Love,
then, is not some squishy, lovey-dovey feeling. God cannot
command a feeling. But he can command a commitment to
the good of another, which is another way to say what love is.

If education is about love, then that means these college years are about much more than obtaining information
or training for a job. Education as ordered and expanded

love means that learning is not just an intellectual act to get smarter or an economic task to get ahead, but a moral act to live into the wholeness of your humanity.

These four years are about discerning what is lovely and deep versus what is ugly and shallow (ordering), as well as growing in your appreciation of what is lovely (expanding). This is the purpose of college. There are things that are more worthy of your time and attention than others. If I love money more than I love my kids (both good things!), my life will be disordered. Part of college is ordering your loves with the deepest, most substantial aspects of life taking primary place. But the other aspect of college is expanding your loves. You may not be drawn to a certain style of music or certain types of books or visual art, but by taking classes on a given subject, the goal is that you would grow in appreciation of what is truly lovely, and so expand what you enjoy and love.

You may come into college thinking, "The sport I play is the best thing in the world. I love it more than anything." I can relate. In college, soccer was my supreme love. It was all I cared about. My emotions rode on winning or losing, and I devoted most of my waking life to being successful. Soccer is a good thing (or substitute soccer for whatever your favorite sport is), but can it hold all of my life? Can success in a sport lead to lifelong happiness? Of course, I thought it could, at least when I was 18. But I quickly discovered it just wasn't so. For one, even if I was as successful as I hoped (and I wasn't), my playing career would last at most 10-15 years past college. I'd be living a majority of my life aimless, unsatisfied, and likely depressed. I love sports, but I had a distorted vision of the good life.

You can replace "soccer" or "sport" with whatever else, and it won't hold up. Will money make you happy? Will career success? Will getting straight A's? Will finding a perfect spouse?

Will achievement? These are all good things but not ultimate things. For example, if I love my job more than I love my family, then my life will be disordered. I won't be functioning how I was intended to function. My life will be a mess. Or if you love your girlfriend or boyfriend more than you love God, then you place unrealistic and crushing expectations on them. Your life will be confused, and your significant other will be exhausted. There are things that are good that need to be loved in the right way, but there are also things that are not to be loved at all. If I love drunkenness or sex outside of marriage, my life will be disordered. You can't rightly love a destructive thing.

Why am I talking about sports, career, and sex? Isn't this book about education? Yes—and a liberal arts education is about cultivating a vision of the good life and knowing how to pursue it. That's why ordering your loves is a central element of education. What are the things worth pursuing and worth loving? There's an ordering of our loves that is necessary for a flourishing or complete life.

There's also an expanding of love that happens in a proper education. Returning to the soccer analogy, I grew to love it. And perhaps you've never grown to love it, because you are still immature and need to be educated in the beauty of soccer. (Just kidding… or am I?) I didn't come out of the womb loving soccer; I was trained to. My parents valued it. I experienced the joy and complexity of it. I spent time doing it. It wasn't always fun, but I grew to see soccer as well worth the effort.

In a similar way, the classroom is, among other things, a training ground for love. You will enroll in plenty of classes that you may dread. You may be one who lights up at the thought of having to complete some complex math problem. I would rather be tortured. Or you may loathe the idea of your first literature class—"Reading novels and writing poetry? No thanks." But the liberal arts—the arts that are made to liberate you—were established to expand your loves: to give you new things to appreciate. I cannot promise that you will love each class you take, but the goal is to at least value those who do enjoy the class. I could never be an accountant, but I am glad there are people who are gifted and passionate about balancing numbers. There is a beauty in balancing numbers.

Education. Ordering and expanding your desires. Love may not be the first thing you thought of when you chose a college, but these formative four or five years will set a trajectory for your next forty. What you love most will shape how you live. What you come to believe will be molded during your college years—for better and for worse. You will be challenged and provoked, poked and prodded. It won't always be comfortable, and it may not always be "fun." But like any truly transformative activity or experience, the hardest things are the ones that are worth the effort in the end.

This love-centered approach to a transformative education has implications for your college years. This is not just some theoretical idea that is nice to know. It impacts how you view your experience in and out of the classroom. Having this view of your college experience will help to mature you into a person who knows how to thrive in life after college.

As a pilgrim, you travel the path that your college sets. The college you attend will have a goal that they want to accomplish, and they will invite you on that journey. In many ways, you don't get to choose your own path—at least not exclusively. The college you choose wants to graduate a certain type of student. And as a student at a given college, it would be helpful to know the path they are ushering you on. At a Christian college, we are likely to be more explicit about our beliefs than the state school down the street. But that public school still functions on values and vision. Usually, no one is going to say, "This is what we believe here at State University."

However, by attending classes, being in the residence halls, and living the practices of a place, you can quickly see what they prioritize as their deepest values. Perhaps the school does not condone any religious conversation in the classroom. They may or may not explicitly say it, but when spirituality is brought up in class, professors or staff neglect that conversation. This experience will frame how you live in the world: you'll pick up the assumption that public conversation is not a place for religion. Or perhaps the school has classes where learning happens but what they really love—what your peers appreciate and the institution pours money into—is the sports program. To be a graduate of this state school, for instance, is to be a football fanatic, dedicated to Saturday game day. This habit will form you as you enter life. You would be malformed to check in at your classes (and then your job), but the really good life is lived on the weekends (usually involving an absurd amount of alcohol and regular, novel sexual interactions). This vision of the good life is what many are led to pursue perhaps without even knowing it. Going to these institutions does not force you into this way of the good life any more than a Christian college forces you to be a Christian, but both encourage a formative direction for you to walk.

Again, a college dean is not going to show up with a document saying, "This is our vision of the good life," or "This is your purpose in life." But a college or university is forming you whether you like it or not. You have chosen a certain moral direction by choosing a Christian college. The good thing about your choice—whether you are a Christian or not—is that we are likely more explicit in what we are aiming at: all Christian institutions want to form you into Christlikeness. Each Christian college will have different flavors about what that means, and how we'll go about it, but at least you know what you're getting into. Christian institutions exist imperfectly. We won't always adequately cultivate this Christ-centered orientation. Some-times, decisions will not reflect the school's mission, and some-times your peers can challenge the college experience. But this truth is inherent in any college education: it will change you!

Conclusion

In this pilgrim life, the destination informs the journey. If life were truly a highway (so sang Rascal Flatts), that would be a fairly dull life: lots of open land and concrete. Sure, life is a journey, but it is going somewhere. Both the journey and the destination matter. But the goal of a highway is to connect you to a particular location. Likewise, it's important to ori-ent our compasses to the right direction as we start out on our college pilgrimage.

Who are you, and what are you here for? Identity and Pur-pose. Understanding these two valuable aspects of existence will help cultivate meaning in the rest of your life. And I think, more than being really smart or super successful, these issues will animate your life. Having a sense of these two aspects is what makes a life meaningful. And good news: this is what the Christian liberal arts college is for.

Discussion Questions

1. The first few days on campus, you were probably asked some version of "Who Are You?" How did you or how would you answer that question?
2. Why did you enroll in college?
3. Do you care about education? Why or why not?
   a. If you don't care about education, do you think you should?
   b. If you do care about education, what reasons would you give to someone that they should care about education?

   c. What would make you care about education, or care about education more?
4. In your own words, how would you define the goal of college? In other words, for what purpose does a college exist?

CHAPTER 2

The Founding: What is a Christian Liberal Arts College, Anyway?

"A liberal education rests on the assumption that nature and human nature do not change very much or very fast and that one therefore needs to understand the past."

Wendell Berry, *The Unsettling of America*

When I was in college, my first roommate was into LARPing. If you know what LARPing is, well, you might be a nerd. If you don't know, LARPing is an acronym for "Live Action Role Playing." Now, LARPing is fine if you're into that sort of thing. But I was most definitely *not* into that sort of thing. So, I dreaded our meeting and living together. But as it turns out, LARPers can be pretty cool people, too. We ended up creating a friendship, mutual understanding, and respect. But I would have never chosen him as a roommate in my dream living situation.

Part of the college experience is participating in classes and spending time outside of the classroom with wildly different kinds of people. Sometimes, these different people will frustrate you because they are so different from you. Other times, their difference will be the very gifts used to change your mind about something important. This experience is one of the great beauties of a college education: being challenged by different perspectives from fellow students who come from different backgrounds.

To take one example: what does it mean to be a Christian school? Some of you have been educated in Christian schools your entire lives, so you may feel like you have a comprehensive answer. "Oh, yeah. That means we pray in class," or "we have a chapel requirement," or "teachers talk about Jesus sometimes." Those answers aren't wrong. Those are some things that Christian colleges tend to do.

For others, this semester is your first experience in a Christian college, and you may have no idea what it means to be in a Christian school. Maybe you think people who go to a Christian college care about arbitrary rules, or they do not have parties, or at least you have to be more secretive about these parties. Or maybe a Christian college is where anti-intellectual, Bible-thumpers send their kids. These are all stereotypes, I know. But we all arrive at our ideas through our own lens and experience, and I want to acknowledge this truth: you have a preconceived notion of what a Christian liberal arts college is. In this section, I want to try to establish some common ground in defining the institution that we are in together.

Putting Christ in the Christian College

Here's a fun fact: Christians founded almost every historic, private institution of higher education in America. Their commitment to love God with all their mind led them to establish the best educational institutions in the country. The historian

William Ringenberg provides an overview of the religious heritage of early American colleges:

> At Harvard the original goal of higher learning was "to know God and Jesus Christ which is eternal life (John 17:3), and therefore to lay Christ in the bottom as the only foundation of all sound knowledge and learning." Yale in early 1700s stated as its primary goal that "every student shall consider the main end of his study to wit to know God in Jesus Christ and answerably to lead a Godly, sober life." Similarly, President Samuel Johnson of Columbia, in a 1754 advertisement, declared that the primary purpose of his college was "to teach and engage the children to know God in Jesus Christ and to love and serve him in all sobriety, godliness, and righteousness of life with a perfect heart and willing mind; and to train them up in all virtuous habits and useful knowledge.[1]

Mostly, these early founders were not just people who called themselves Christians who started these things called colleges, rather Jesus was central to their understanding and commitment to education. They wanted Jesus to permeate the entire learning enterprise. These early colleges exercised faith as fundamental to their founding and purpose.

Later, as these colleges drifted from their founding mission, other colleges were created. These new institutions defined themselves by their Christian "worldview." Because of your parents, community, and country, you are formed to view the world a certain way, and sometimes it is in reaction to the way your parents raised you or your community formed you. But the truth of the matter is that you see in your own unique way. That's called your "worldview"—and you will likely hear a lot about worldview in your four years in college. What ultimate values do you have? Where do they come from? What do you believe? The answer to those questions will affect how you view the world—hence, what is often called your "worldview."

If I can summarize the Christian worldview as clearly and succinctly as I can, here it is: God created a good world filled with wonders, and he endowed the pinnacle of his creation, men and women, with the incredible capacity to image Him. As such, humans are not just hunks of flesh, but embodied souls created by God and given meaning and purpose. You have inherent dignity and worth, and we all have equal dignity and worth because we are made in the image of God. Moreover, God has gifted this special creation of humankind with the ability to comprehend his revelation. God is the unifying essence that holds the world together, and by which we understand the world and ourselves. But bad news—and you may have heard this—humankind sinned through our common parents, Adam and Eve. Satan, disguised as a serpent, entered the perfect harmony of the garden, and challenged God's truth, authority, and trustworthiness. Rather than believe what God had said, our forebearers trusted the serpent's lies about significance and meaning. They sought provision, wisdom, and pleasure apart from God. And like our first parents, we can be confused about truth and falsehood, goodness and evil, beauty and ugliness. Now, the task of knowing is distorted and twisted—who can we trust? What will bring us happiness and a life of harmony? We are alienated from God, each other, the natural world, and even ourselves. What theologians call the Fall seeps into every crevice of our lives and every facet of the creation.

But, of course, the good news: Jesus came to redeem those under the curse of sin. He lived the life we were meant to live and died the death we deserved, so that we may live rightly with God, empowered by the Holy Spirit. This is a gift from God. We did not deserve it or earn it. By grace we have been saved. This is the central truth of the universe. Jesus' life, death, and resurrection restores trustworthiness—if God did not spare his Son but sent Him for us, shouldn't we trust what he says? What good thing would he withhold from us having already given us the most precious gift?

And now we wait for his return to fully restore all things. Right now, things are still marked by the Fall. Marriages are broken. Learning disorders exist. Cancer kills people. Children die. This is not the way things are supposed to be! So, God calls us to join Him in renewing the world. In the Lord's Prayer, we say, "Your kingdom come, your will be done, on earth as it is in heaven," and we participate with God in making that reality true even as we wait for the full restoration of all things. In many ways, this call to re-make and re-store the world in line with God's coming kingdom is what you are called to—your "vocation." As you decide to pursue your major and career, ask the question: what would it look like for kingdom life to be present in the corporate boardroom or by the hospital bed or industrial engineering?

Creation. Fall. Redemption. Restoration. These are the four major turns in the story of the world according to a Christian worldview. This story we find ourselves in is not about you. This story is about Jesus reconciling the world to Himself, and He invites you to be a participant in it. This story should animate Christian colleges. Christian colleges seek to make this story front and center in everything we do because we think this is the most important and truest story in the world—a story that can transform your life and a story that can transform the world—including our academic subjects.

Other people will be storied differently. One way to "use" the Christian worldview is to evaluate other worldviews. How does a Christian worldview compare to a secular, a progressive/conservative, a postmodern, or a nihilist world-view? How does a Christian vision of the good life differ from a postmodern vision? Or how does a modern worldview's understanding of truth or personhood compare to a Christian worldview? These are worthwhile (and interesting!) discussions to have.

You will find that you may disagree with some professors at your school, and some of your professors disagree with each other. For example, I'm Anglican, and I work with Baptists, Presbyterians, and Pentecostals. Other disagreements may be more substantial—the way we vote or in what ways Christian faith should be integrated into psychology. A Christian worldview does not mean we all think alike or believe the same things, but it does mean we attempt to answer questions acknowledging that Jesus informs our thinking and learning. We are all trying to bring every thought captive to obey Christ (2 Cor. 10:5). And the Christian college is one path where we can work out our Christian thinking in the context of a like-minded community.

A thorough and robust Christian worldview should be the animating story of a Christian college—it makes a difference in what we believe as opposed to another institution. A worldview could be a doctrinal statement that is in some handbook that you are supposed to read and won't, or that you have to take New Testament or Christian Doctrine in your general education requirements. Whichever way worldview filters down, a Christian college attempts to pass this story on to you. However, a Christian college is more than its worldview or doctrinal statements because Christianity is not merely an intellectual system. Postures and practices also matter.

Here's what I mean: a school could have all the right biblical beliefs, but if the professors, staff, and administrators are bitter, angry, and stubborn, would that reflect the light of Jesus? The obvious answer is no. Or, what if the institution admitted students that were likely to fail? The college gets the paycheck, but at what expense and according to what ethic? And if they do admit low achieving or under prepared students—how much help is going to support those students? Being a Christian and living out of an intentional Christian worldview gives us a certain way of being in the world and gives us insight. A Christian college should reflect a posture of Christianity—one marked by the fruit of the Spirit: love, joy, peace, patience, kindness, gentleness, and self-control. Of course, colleges won't live this perfectly, as all colleges will fall short at upholding precise doctrinal truth. But the posture matters, as well as the content. Christians should be marked by Christlikeness in their character—and repentance when they fail.

Another aspect to note in a Christian college is its practices. Chapel is a practice. Bible study in the residence halls is a practice. Starting class in prayer is a practice. But so are grading, parties, football games, etc. All of these are practices that shape you—some for better, some for worse. If you were to take an audit of your Christian college, what practices are scripted for you? What practices are emphasized? What do those emphasized practices say about what the school values? What do your classroom practices say about what the teacher values? Is it all about grades? Is Christianity a tack on at the end of a few lessons, or does the faith play itself out in how the teacher treats the class and how the class treats each other?

One of the things I do on the first day of class is start with community building rather than going over the syllabus right away.[2] Now, I hate "ice-breakers" as much as the next introvert. If I start with the syllabus, what am I truly saying matters most over the semester? Subtly, the practice of covering the syllabus communicates that what matters in this class is how well you do on the assignments. But I view my classes as a community of scholars. To arrive at truth, we need each other's voices, and we need to trust one another to share our honest opinions and reflections. The practice of starting with getting to know one another is a way that my Christianity affects my teaching practice. Simply knowing a student's name could be a practice that cultivates a deeply Christian classroom that is shaped by love and relational bonds rather than transactions.

All of these—content, posture, and practices—form and shape a distinctively Christian college as opposed to a Christian college in name only.

The Liberal (and Liberating) Arts

I know what many of you are thinking: "Oh. The liberal arts? Those are the unnecessary classes I'm forced to take before I can take the classes I want to take. Great. This should be fun." I want to try to persuade you to think differently about the courses you'll take to start your college journey. Rather than viewing these general education classes as disconnected from your major, I want to argue that these classes are the foundation of your education.

The liberal arts go way back. Before Christianity, there were the liberal arts. Historically, there are two parts of a liberal arts education: the trivium and quadrivium. The trivium is comprised of grammar, logic, and rhetoric (tri=three). These are seen as steps to learning. First, a student needs to learn language and how words are put together in basic building blocks—that's grammar. Then a student progresses to understand the reasoning of the basic building blocks— that's logic. Finally, they move to persuasively communicate what they have learned—that's rhetoric. This process is how we discover truth—which is what a good education is about—and what I think we all want is to discern truth from error. The ancients believed that the soul was properly formed through these subjects.

The quadrivium includes astronomy, mathematics, geometry, and music (quad=four). These studies focused on the content of mathematical truth to prepare for discovering truth with clarity of thought and wonder. It's how we discover and investigate the external world. Your general studies or core requirements are built on this foundation: the humanities (trivium) and the scientific arts (quadrivium). These seven categories of subjects compose the liberal arts curriculum. In essence, these subjects deal with three relations: humankind relating to themselves, humankind relating to others, and humankind relating to their natural environment and surroundings.

Below, I want to provide two main reasons for why the liberal arts are a most necessary foundation. First, the liberal arts have the potential to set you free. Second, the liberal arts form a well-rounded person.

Free Person

Historically, the liberal arts have a counterpart called the servile arts. The servile arts are those subjects that serve a purpose other than itself. Here's what I mean: you learn accounting not for the good of accounting, but so you can calculate profit and loss. Or you learn family dynamics for the purpose of wisdom in counseling. For the most part, your major classes are servile arts: They are intended to make you employable, to cultivate a certain skill or trade, and to specialize. And these matter!

In contrast, the liberal arts are goods in and of themselves. Whether these disciplines make you employable or not, they broaden your perspective, deepen your understanding, and help you appreciate their beauty. There's this deep part of you called the soul, and the liberal arts cultivate this deep part of you. While the servile arts are concerned with the body—making things, money, profits, food—the liberal arts serve the soul—that intangible aspect of your existence. As such, the liberal arts are a general base that serves wisdom rather than more specific skills to serve some other end.

To be clear, there is nothing wrong with the servile arts. We need them because we need food, shelter, and a job, and they can be pursued with dignity and for the sake of restoring God's world. But education is more than career training. We need a broad base of knowledge to see how our specific interests may fit within the whole. Modern education has produced people with narrow specialization that neglects how a specialized interest may affect the broader picture. Your knowledge will always be partial, but a liberal arts education is meant to expand your vision.

Furthermore, the liberal arts are meant to cultivate a free citizenship. In order not to be a slave to tyranny, your circumstance, or just what other people tell you, the liberal arts were developed to shape a free people. While the servile arts are based on survival, the liberal arts ask a more fundamental question: Why even survive at all? What's the point? And I think that is what you want in an education: to reliably pursue the truth, to discern goodness from evil, and to pursue the beautiful life rather than an ugly one. These liberal arts can refine your thinking, cultivate wisdom and virtue, and so make you free.

In today's world, freedom is often discussed as "freedom from." "I am free," you may think, which means you have no constraints or binds that prevent you from doing something. That is good and well. But there is also a more ancient definition of freedom that includes "freedom to." Are you free to pursue the good in life? Are you free from poor thinking or bad habits that prevent you from desiring the best in life? I may tell you, "You are free to play Mozart on the piano." In a real sense, you are free to walk over to the piano, sit down, and bang on the keys. No one is stopping you. But only a trained piano player is free to play Mozart in the "freedom to" sense. The liberal arts invite you to pursue a meaningful life by developing these essential human interests, so that you're not a slave to money, the economy, or even your own selfish interests. These subjects function as food for the soul to enlarge and expand your appreciation for the world.

My support of the liberal arts is not to pit the liberal arts against the servile arts or the body against the soul. The liberal arts need the servile arts, and the servile arts need the liberal arts. We are embodied souls and undividedly so. We can't separate ourselves so cleanly. I'm advocating for a type of education where mechanics can be poets and philosophers can be carpenters—a truly liberal education where men and women are raised as wise and skilled free people. Why not teach theology alongside shop class?[3]

Whole Person

Secondly, a liberal arts education invites you to be more fully human. Some have termed this a *humane* education—one that resonates with the deepest parts of who we are. Now, you may be thinking, this task seems unnecessary—as unnecessary as learning how to think. The fact that you are breathing and reading this page is evidence that you are both thinking and human. How can I be *more* human? But the liberal arts are about more than mere existence. Instead, they ask, how does one exist in the deepest, truest way? Or to bring a Christian term into the discussion, how can I image God in a fuller and clearer way? The liberal arts provide teachers and texts to help along the path.

The liberal arts reflect a well-rounded education. You will be drawn to certain subjects more than others. You may find the idea of being forced to take a math class absolute drudgery. You may think there's no better punishment than having to take an art class or write a short story. But here's the truth: you need it. To be whole, you need full cultivation of all your general capabilities. You will be malformed if you neglect your full humanity. The liberal arts holistically shape you by stretching you to reach your full potential: thinking precisely, developing virtue, appreciating beauty. We will never arrive at a full, holistic knowledge—that belongs to God alone. But as we learn, we weave together the fragments we do understand as we receive more fragments. A liberal arts education seeks to fit the fragments within the whole.

I won't bore you with my whole college story, but I did not choose well. As an 18-year-old, I didn't have the knowledge, experience, or wisdom to know what was best for me. I chose a specialized education that narrowly prepared me for the job I wanted. Nobody suggested (or required) the classes that were best for me, so I chose what I thought would interest me. In most every way, I chose the easy path. As a result, I'm still catching up in living into my full humanity. Why read literature when I'm not going to be a writer or study biology when I'm not going to be doctor? I lacked the imagination of what truly matters—that literature can form my imagination and biology can hone my interest in the natural world. And I am worse off for it. I only developed one aspect of my humanity—like a weightlifter who only does bicep curls but neglects leg day.

Like me, you need guides to help you be a well-rounded person. As humans, we do not have all the resources within ourselves to fully develop. Most of us, if left to ourselves, would likely pick what is easy, what you like, and what comes naturally. But what if the flourishing life does not come by what is easy, but by what is best? Often, what is easy and what is best are at odds. Sometimes, they align but more often you need to be challenged and sharpened, which means being stretched by things uncomfortable or "over your head." And those who have gone before you have paved a path— whether that be an ancient text or a teacher. They are not without flaws or free from critique, but perhaps there is something there to help you.

As such, the well-curated liberal arts introduce you to what many consider the best of what has been thought, so that you can live better and think clearer and more broadly. And by thinking better and clearer, the goal is for you to love more fully and broadly. Because we share a common humanity, we can be helped, assisted, sharpened, and challenged by much of what has gone before us knowing that past writers and thinkers experienced the same human longings, questions, and distresses as we do. By seeing their answers, we may better understand our own.

Let me temper my love and passion for the liberal arts a bit. The liberal arts education does not equate to being a free and whole person. I am a Christian, after all. The liberal arts do not possess the power to save. There are many people who have gone through the educational system who remain bound and diminished. Rather, the liberal arts are an invitation to cultivate these deepest parts of us by asking enduring and important questions—for the Christian and non-Christian alike. I believe the local church is the most important institution in the world. The church holds the gospel: the power of God unto salvation for everyone who believes (Rom. 1:16).

You can't beat that! But let me suggest that the second most important institution in the world is the Christian liberal arts college. It is worth investing in, caring about, nurturing—and yes, even paying for.

A Faithfully Christian Liberal Arts College

If a liberal arts education is meant to develop our full humanity through exploration of the true, the beautiful, and the good, we must ask: What is true? Or good? Or beautiful? And why these three? In the classical tradition from ancient Greece, these are called the "transcendentals," because they reflect the transcendent—the aspect of creation that all reality shares. The transcendent is the "Idea" to which all things should conform—humanity included. In Christianity, God is the Transcendental: the One who is all true, all good, and all beautiful. The Transcendent God created us in his image, to reflect his truth, beauty, and goodness. We reflect this image in varying degrees and in varying ways, but God proposes the path forward: to reflect Him as fully as we can.

A Christian liberal arts education is meant to cultivate a particular vision of humanity: reflecting God. Since we are made in God's image or likeness, then we try to more closely reflect that original image. If a Christian education is about taking the Christian story seriously, and a liberal arts education is about developing our humanity, then a Christian liberal arts education is about a particular vision of humanity—namely, one that images God.

Hugh of St. Victor was an early Christian educator who said as much in his discussion of the purpose of education. Hugh served the school at St. Victor in France from 1120 to 1141. He saw the nature of education as a formative task. Drawing on the biblical tradition before him, he insisted that the goal of education was to reconnect students with the image of God that was marred by the Fall. He writes,

> This, then, is what the arts are concerned with, this is what they intend, namely, to restore within us the divine likeness, a likeness which to us is a form, but to God is his nature. The more we are conformed to the divine nature, the more do we possess Wisdom, for then there begins to shine forth in us what has forever existed in the divine Idea or Pattern, coming and going in us but standing changeless in God.[4]

A Christian liberal arts education is meant to restore a divine likeness in us that conforms to God. Certainly, an education does not guarantee this, nor is a college the only place where divine restoration happens. But a Christian liberal arts school has the resources to pursue the path of student formation in exploring the true, good, and beautiful. These transcendentals reflect the transcendent God in whose image we are made and whose likeness we desire.

In the Christian liberal arts, there are multiple pilgrimages you make. You journey backward into history to read about formative people and places. You journey inward into your own soul when you study psychology, philosophy, and literature. You journey to the outside world as you study biology, chemistry, and natural science. You journey "upward" toward God in studying theology. The Christian liberal arts invite you on these ventures and explorations.

Problems in Paradise

I hope you find this vision of a Christian liberal arts education compelling. I hope you may even be excited to start your college journey, realizing the rich tradition you have entered.

However, I would be lying to say that this vision has ever been perfectly put into practice. This vision of a Christian liberal arts education is a goal we pursue—not something Christian colleges have ever perfectly established. For as much as a historic Christian education contributed to our understanding of education, the past has its issues.

First, a Christian education can be limiting. If Christianity is separated from the liberal arts, Christians can tend to think that the Bible is all that matters—like Jonathan in the introduction who thought the Bible was the only worthwhile subject. "Why busy yourself with 'secular' study when you can study the Bible? Everything in there is true." This line of thinking reflects an education where only the Bible matters, where we reject other sources of truth. It's true that the Bible is key to our understanding of life and our place in the world, but other subjects help our understanding of truth. Theologically, there's an idea called "common grace." There's special grace bestowed to Christians via the Bible—it's particular revelation to the church. But what can be known about God is not just in the Bible but also through the created order and through nature. Common grace is the idea that even those who do not believe in God have the capacity to know things about the world and God. Because God bestowed this common grace upon all humanity, non-Christian scholars can help us think clearer and more fully. For example, psychologists or neurologists can help us understand the effects of trauma. Botanists can help us see the complexity and beauty of plant life. We should celebrate common grace truths wherever they are found and not reduce a Christian education to merely a Bible class.

Moreover, a Christian education can often be reduced to worldview training, assuming that once you get the Christian story of the world, then you are done. But knowing the story is not some magic bullet to cure all ills of bad thinking or bad

practice. At times, reducing education to information can si-
phon off a holistic approach to education. Yes, we need the
story, but we also need the practices and postures that the
story inspires. The metanarrative, the big story of creation,
fall, redemption, and restoration—it frames our education.
But an education involves more than knowing the Bible's story.

For example, in the past people who believed all the right
things about the Bible practiced an education that denied
people the truth of what the Bible claims. Though the church
affirmed that God created all people in the image of God,
education was limited to the privileged, particularly "gentle-
men." In other words, if you look around at your classmates,
somewhere between 50-70% would not have been allowed
to receive an education a few centuries ago. Any woman or
minority you see would not have had access to an education
in the early, elite Christian colleges like Harvard, Princeton,
or Yale. The only humanity worth cultivating was privileged,
white males.

Christian education was open to the divine and mysterious. However, it is important to remember that, at times,
Christians criticized technological advancement or creative
solutions to problems in preference for the status-quo. Yes,
tradition is a good, stabilizing force, but this good vision
of education was cast in a world where illiteracy, poverty,
disease, and slavery ran rampant. Innovation did great good
to the church and the world. Modernization led to the diagnosis and treatment of disease, expanding transportation,
and the advance of technology. Electricity, farming efficien-
cies, and airplane travel all came with the modernization of
society. God does call his followers to faithfully pass on and
transmit the faith, but his call is also to extend his kingdom's
reign "as the waters cover the sea" (Hab. 2:14). Innovation

and creativity were sparked in modern advancement, which we ought to celebrate.

Lastly, if you challenged these beliefs of Christianity, then you were labeled a heretic. And what do you do with heretics? You burn them at the stake. I'm glad we have moved past that stage where we kill people who disagree with us.

For all these reasons, there was not some Christian golden age of education. I am not advocating for a return to an ancient past but to rescue the good of the Christian liberal arts tradition while we discern the errors.

Conclusion

Writing in *Touchstone Magazine,* Bret J. Saunders provides a great definition of education. He suggests that "education is different from job training. Education is for making you the kind of person who will pursue the true, the good, and the beautiful regardless of how you 'make a living' and how much you make. Education is the shaping of the imagination and the filling of the heart."[5] But for various reasons, I am guessing this is not the vision of education with which you came into college.

In the chapters that follow, I will give a very broad history of colleges in the United States to consider how education has been reduced from this holistic task. In essence, the goal of education has been cheapened, and with it, your own humanity has been degraded.

Here is your task in your four years at a Christian liberal arts college: to shape your imagination and fill your heart—to become a different person. These years will make you wonder and encourage you to ask a lot of questions. At the end of those questions, the goal is to pursue stable, lasting things—those aspects of creation that are good, true, and beautiful. Try on ideas and see how they fit. Challenge your classmates.

Listen to them. As you do, you will develop and grow in virtue. This is the goal of the liberal arts.

Discussion Questions

1. Before reading this chapter, what were your ideas about the purpose of a Christian education?
2. What is a "Christian worldview?" How does a Christian worldview affect education? How might a different worldview change the way you think about education?
3. In your own words, what is the purpose of the liberal arts, and why are they valuable to your education?
4. Describe an experience where you learned something from someone who you may not have liked or agreed with on anything else? What happened? What was that conversation or experience like? What did that teach you?
5. Reflect on this quote from Bret Saunders: "Education is different from job training. Education is for making you the kind of person who will pursue the true, the good, and the beautiful regardless of how you 'make a living' and how much you make. Education is the shaping of the imagination and the filling of the heart."[6] At this point, do you agree or disagree? Why? How would this reshape how you imagine your college years?

Notes

1. William Ringenberg, *The Christian College: A History of Protestant Higher Education in America* (Grand Rapids: Baker Academic, 2006), 38.

2. I get this from David Smith in *On Christian Teaching: Practicing Faith in the Classroom* (Grand Rapids: Eerdmans Press, 2018).

3. For more, read Matthew Crawford's *Shop Class as Soul Craft: An Inquiry into the Value of Work* (New York: Penguin Books, 2010).

4. Hugh of St. Victor, *The Didascalion of Hugh of Saint Victor: A Medieval Guide to the Arts*, trans. Jerome Taylor (New York: Columbia University Press, 1991), 61.

5. Bret J. Saunders, "The Worlds in a Grain of Sand," *Touchstone Magazine*, January/February 2017, 19.

6. Ibid.

CHAPTER 3

College for Thinkers:
The City of Big Brains

"The aim, as in all theological and biblical exploration,
is not to replace love with knowledge. Rather, it is to
keep love focused upon its true object."

NT Wright, *The Day the Revolution Began*

"The heart has its reasons of which reason knows nothing."

Blaise Pascal, *Pensées*

In the novel *Hard Times*, Charles Dickens describes a modern classroom. Professor Gradgrind stands at the front. In front of him, each student is assigned a number. He calls them little pitchers because he dispenses facts into their brains until they're full. Then, for a test, the pitchers empty their mind receptacles in a fashion fit for the teacher. Infamously, Gradgrind proclaims, "Now what I want is facts. Teach these boys and girls nothing but facts."

Toward the beginning of the story, the class receives a new student. Sissy is her given name, but her class name is #20. The class finds out that her dad works with circus horses, which is a silly, low-class job compared to the self-respecting group of middle-class students. Professor Gradgrind has a simple question for Sissy to start: What is a horse?

Sissy struggles to answer, and she stumbles over her words. A horse is a horse, she thinks. She cannot answer the question in a way that is satisfying to Professor Gradgrind. Finally fed up, Gradgrind calls on a boy, Bitzer. Bitzer responds, "Quadruped. Graminivorous. Forty teeth, namely twenty-four grinders, four eye-teeth, and twelve incisive. Sheds coat in the spring; in marshy countries, sheds hoofs, too. Hoofs hard but requiring to be shod with iron. Age known by marks in mouth."[1] "Ah ha!" So, one assumes, "Here, we have a true answer of what a horse is."

Now, who really knows a horse? Sissy—the one who was raised with them, had worked with them, and intimately relates to them—or Bitzer, who memorized answers in a book? The irony is that Sissy's knowledge was denied, while the book learning of Bitzer was commended. Learning that is rooted in relation or affection is rejected, while learning that stems from a distance is praised. Indeed, as Dickens' title frames it, education has fallen on "hard times."

If I were a betting man, I'd bet that the above parable could serve as a fitting picture of how you have experienced education in the K-12 classroom, and how you may currently view education. Imagine a classroom set up: the teacher is at the front, because he has all the facts. You are an individual at an individual desk learning from the expert in front of you. Community, relationships, and connection are not encouraged. You are an individual, little pitcher. You are a "brain-on-a-stick."[2] We're all prone to Gradgrind now.

The temptation in the City of Big Brains is to find your worth in your grade point average. In this city, the person deemed smartest is the worthiest. Success is measured by who has proven good enough to be the valedictorian. There's no time for play; only study. Relationships may get in the way. Depend on no one. While people are out having fun, you need to be preparing for the next test.

The Shaping of the College for Thinkers

In the previous chapter, I mentioned that nearly every college in America started with Christian faith commitments. Well, you probably know this, but Harvard, Yale, and Brown do not identify as Christian colleges anymore. What happened?

The Rise of the Mind

There was a historical era called the Enlightenment in Europe during the 18th century. As the name suggests, it's when humanity decided it had become "enlightened" by the power of reason and observation. Shedding religious knowledge and tradition, the use of the mind and the senses became dominant in this period. Two important thinkers that shaped this development were René Descartes and Immanuel Kant. This section will serve as a partial history as we look at their main ideas.

Descartes' story starts in fear, anxiety, and crisis. He was on a quest for truth—a task with which colleges and universities will resonate. The question he sought to answer was, "How can humans know anything with certainty?" Even a statement such as, "I am writing at my desk" was riddled with doubt, because he could be dreaming or imagining that situation. Perhaps he thought he existed in a dream state or in self-deception. So, here's what Descartes decided to do:

he went to his room for several days in order to think his way through his conundrum. The idea that emerged from Descartes' wrestling with doubt was doubt itself. The only reliable thing he could be certain of was doubt. Doubt is, fundamentally, an activity of the mind. Hence the famous saying of Descartes, "I think, therefore I am." He knows he exists because he is thinking. Notice what this says about humanity: you are a thinking-thing. You are not a soul; you are a mind. Your own personal reasoning ability is the only reliable source of truth. Other people or guides are not reliable; feelings are not reliable. Only thinking is reliable. As such, the mind is the central element of humankind, the only reliable guide.

Since the mind is the authority disconnected from tradition and the divine, education starts in doubt. In the older conception, education started in wonder. You would ask, "Wow. That's strange. Why is it like that?" and you might go to sources with wisdom to find out. In the Enlightenment, education tends to start in doubt, where a student should separate feeling, connection, and authority from a subject. The student is encouraged to appeal to only reason for truth. Do not trust what other people tell you—whether other people are your parents, your religious authorities, or your friends. What's important is thinking for yourself as an individual. Hence, you have individual desks to do your individual thinking. As shown in the story of *Hard Times*, Sissy's appreciation of horses proved her downfall. She loved horses, so she was not "objective." She did not learn the facts from the "experts."

Growth to Maturity

Following Descartes in the Enlightenment, the mind and reason rose as the primary authority. Later on, a German philosopher by the name of Immanuel Kant entered the scene. As an inheritor of the Enlightenment tradition, he writes:

> Enlightenment is man's emergence from his self-imposed immaturity. Immaturity is the inability to use one's own understanding without the guidance of another. This immaturity is self-imposed if its cause lies not in lack of understanding but in indecision and lack of courage to use one's own mind without another's guidance. The motto of enlightenment is therefore: *sapere aude!* Have the courage to use your own understanding![3]

This charge became a rallying cry for the College of Thinkers: dare to know and dare to think for yourself. Immaturity keeps a student from understanding. What we need to do is put on our big boy and big girl pants and grow up. Leave behind the authorities and guides of your past. The individual becomes their own scientific, religious, and ethical authority. Kant's philosophy identifies reason as playing a salvific role by rescuing humanity from ignorance. Your mind will save you. With no authorities, science becomes the guiding principle for education. If you cannot see, taste, touch, smell, or measure it, then it cannot be certain. The scientific person is often most valued in today's society.

Trials in the City of Big Brains

These two revolutions inspired by Descartes and Kant resulted in a change of belief system in much of Western culture. "Secular" is often a term for those exhibiting "no belief" or in opposition to belief. So, secular school, secular music, or secular culture is deemed as the opposite of Christian school, music, or culture. However, this turn to the secular is not a change to no belief but to a different belief.

The authority they claim—science—comes with its own set of doctrines. Science, with its own purpose and meaning, became an objective standard including its own set of ethics and virtues. The new task of the university was to connect science to the formation of students. The purpose of a university after this secular shift was no longer developing the image of God within the student; rather, the new goal was the formation of the scientific person by the cultivation of the rational mind alone.

The scientific revolution culminated with the work and thought of Charles Darwin. If you remember Darwin, he's the one who developed the theory of evolution. According to Darwin, rather than animals created for a goal or purpose, everything changes based on naturalistic causes. In the Darwinist worldview, there is no final goal determined by God or greater purpose for humanity. We are subject to chance evolutionary changes and developments. In Darwin, everything is merely physical and scientific. Those after Darwin explained everything by naturalistic causes and random change. There is nothing inherently dignifying about the soul of humans. We have evolved and matured out of religious belief. The way we learn is by impartation of scientific facts through the scientific method. To arrive at certainty, we need to be able to test and objectively verify. It is easier to measure and test mathematical proofs than to say what makes a life worth living. That's just your opinion, dude.

The Enlightenment and the Darwinian Revolution frame the college ethos in the City of Big Brains as existing within a materialistic, naturalistic explanation for all things. Instead of as a soul, humans are construed as purely mechanical minds—hunks of material flesh. There is no higher power and no spiritual nature inherent in humanity. Rather, there is brain chemistry, consciousness, and individual reason.

The result from these thinkers is what has been called the "elephantiasis of reason"[4] in the university. Elephantiasis is a disease that morphs a part of the body to become inflated and overgrown. Imagine a ginormous head with a little body. In essence, that is the vision of humanity in many modern universities as they seek to educate minds. No longer does higher education view its task as forming human persons made in the image of God. After all, the image of God does not exist since the divine cannot be rationally proven. There are no God-given gifts—no understanding, deep knowledge, or real purpose—instead, you are only a mind made for individual reasoning.

As mentioned in the previous chapter, where the ancient age sought "freedom to," Enlightenment University sought "freedom from."[5] True freedom was found where there were no limitations. When I ask students what freedom means, they usually mean something like "nobody can tell me what to do" or "I can do whatever I want." But that's only one kind of freedom. That's freedom from constraint. Many contemporary students lack the vocabulary or concepts of being "free to" or "free for" a positive good. Who is really free to make a hundred three-pointers in a row: a professional basketball player or me? Answer: the basketball player. Sure, I can heave a basketball up toward the general vicinity of the hoop. No one is stopping me. But that freedom to do the positive good means the constraint of time, practice, and effort that I have not given. This latter aspect of freedom is all but gone from our modern conceptions.

In many ways, science became the religion of the day. Again, these movements were not an abandonment of belief but a change of beliefs, away from a historic Christianity to a secularized faith in science alone. A main shortcoming in the scientism of the university is the belief that the university is a mere transmitter of knowledge. However, the university legitimizes and authorizes knowledge as well. The mind, along with the university, is loaded with a dogma of its own that it attempts to pass on to the next generation. In the age of reason, the dogma or doctrine was scientism. I am all for science, and the scientific method. It helps regulate fields of inquiry and offers evidence for trials. But scientism takes these good scientific developments and makes them ultimate and supreme. Like Isabel that I mentioned in the Introduction, if you can't prove it by science, then it's not valuable. Or if it's not on the test, who cares?

Perhaps the University of Virginia provides an apt visual picture of this development toward scientific knowledge. Instead of the chapel as the center of the college campus, founder Thomas Jefferson placed the library in this prominent position. The modern university picks up on this intellectual vision of the college. Now, faith and God are private realities, sequestered to some corner of campus (if on campus at all). More information is the central concern in the City for Big Brains.

Dangers in the City of Big Brains

You have inherited a vision of learning. I want you to see that nothing happens in a vacuum. You have come to understand "the way things are" because "the way things are" is the way things have been for hundreds of years. As much good as the Enlightenment and Scientific Revolution have brought, they also deform the Christian student. In what ways?

Fragmentation and Specialization

In many ways, the story of the university in America is one of segmentation and fragmentation. Christianity gave a big story in which humanity fit, its purpose was clear, and its knowledge was whole. God was the one unifying force of the "uni"-versity. The curriculum and classes made sense as they made sense under God's pattern and design. Theology was the "Queen of the Sciences"—the crowning subject. But in the College for Thinkers, instead of a united vision for the nature of humanity and the ends to which they have been made, there exists a growing specialization in education. There is no subject that unifies the curriculum. You may feel this as you take your liberal arts classes. They seem like a hodge-podge of information without any unifying purpose or connected theory. You sort of pass through them, but how does math and literature connect? I have a friend who describes the modern view of education as similar to Pokémon cards. You read a book, and then you collect that to show off to others. Or you get an A in a class and put it in your binder of cards to prove yourself a truly educated person. But there's no connection between them. Education is basically a game to collect pieces of disconnected pieces of information. There isn't a common knowledge in which students are introduced in the heritage of the liberal arts.

To be fair, we need specialization. College research is about going deep into a small sliver of a field of knowledge. Learning requires you to know something, and earning a doctorate requires you be the expert on something new. This move is another turn to reduce knowledge to mere facts and information. We tend to lack the general knowledge which can connect the small bits of information to the larger whole. Why does any small piece of information matter in the grand scheme of things? We need the broad-based learning of the liberal arts to make sense of our growing specialized knowledge. Education properly understood is about connecting the fragments we do learn, and we need a whole picture to map our knowledge.

Is Learning Really the Christian Problem?

To critique reason seems like I am recommending a shift to premodern, antiquated faith. Do I really want to turn to some ancient path where new knowledge seems unimportant? Am I some sort of weird guy who wants to reject the advances of technology brought about by science?

Maybe you think the problem of evangelical Christians is their lack of intellectual engagement. On the one hand, as Mark Noll once stated in his book: "The scandal of the evangelical mind is that there is not much of an evangelical mind."[6] For many, evangelicals need more—not less. The critique of anti-intellectualism among evangelicals is embarrassingly true; by and large, we have a low concern for the intellectual life. If anything, it seems Christians need a renewal of intellectual activity—not a retreat.

On the other hand, some Christians often view theology like we're in the City of Big Brains. We think having the right abstract theology will lead to change of behavior. Doctrinal precision is said to result in spiritual maturity. J. P. Moreland illustrates this when he writes, "The mind is the soul's primary vehicle for making contact with God, and it plays a fundamental role in the process of human maturation and change, including spiritual transformation."[7] Is the Christian mind inflated like the elephantiasis of the university, or is it suffering decay from lack of use?

In short, yes—both are true. On the one hand, evangelicals tend to disregard the life of the mind by succumbing to shallow answers and explanations. Our churches can be prone to letting emotions be the authority on truth. So, when asked to defend why something is right, many will say, "Well, I feel it be true." Or you can hear classmates start sentences with, "I feel…" Emotions can be a guide in evangelical Christianity—oftentimes in misleading ways. On the other hand,

Christians can also inflate the role of the mind for the means of growth. While I do not want to retreat from intellect, I do want to place reason in its proper place. In the biblical understanding, having more information is not the foundational means of transformation. Knowing and learning is a holistic endeavor that is not the opposite of feeling, body, or connection. Change does not happen by information being transferred to the mind. Charles Taylor describes the tradition following René Descartes as offering a "monological consciousness."[8] In other words, it's my conscience and thoughts that determine truth apart from my body and other people. Understanding comes from me alone. But we learn with our body, and we know with others. Education, whether reading or listening, is a social task. The idea of a solitary, autonomous reasoner is a myth. As much as "thinking for oneself" is promoted, the task is impossible. Thinking is always a response or reaction to someone else's thought or idea. As such, thinking starts in and is shaped by a community. Your task is to find a good community to think with, be challenged by, and be supported in. As such, Descartes' tradition limits and reduces the nature of human knowing and education.

Moreover, one of the main consequences of the Enlightenment is the loss of wonder. Facts become the main point of education. Those with explanations are the experts. Therefore, the task of the university is to discover what is measurable in the most efficient manner. This development has been devastating the purpose of the university because most things worth knowing are neither measurable nor efficient. This pursuit of "measurability" stifles both humanity and imagination. How do you measure a good life? How do you manufacture wisdom? These ultimate questions are deeper than can be answered by scientific facts. When I talk about a vision of education developing a whole person, I hope that excites you.

You know what will kill an education? Making it about grades or standardized testing. As you probably know better than I can tell you, when learning is just about getting the correct letter on a report card, then your passion is not in learning itself but in getting the grade.

People like Sissy can teach us a lot about horses even without knowing the textbook answer. Sissy's knowledge arose from real caring. So often, modern schooling deadens a student's interest in passionate learning and real engagement in favor of "objectivity." The goal is for you to become disengaged and uninterested. You may resonate with this story. You've seen kids be curious, wonder, and ask questions, but after a few years of schooling, the spark of the imagination dwindles. Rather than expanding and fanning the sparks of wonder, the College for Thinkers tends to cheapen and so deaden the imagination. All that's left is a humanity reduced to computing capacities.

Conclusion

Perhaps the City for Big Brains is a particular danger to type-A students, those students that are achievement-oriented and want to be the best. I was not necessarily a hard worker when it came to school, but I wanted to do well. I had other interests that I cared about succeeding in (sports, women, etc.), but I did well enough to get by. But my goal in the classroom was about my own individual success. I did not care about helping others learn or spending time developing relationships. I was in college to earn grades through my individual effort and intelligence—or at least my ability to memorize facts. I did not think my learning or classroom time made any difference on how I approached life or others.

When I was discerning a call to ministry and pursuing advanced degrees, I applied my mental energy to acquiring knowledge of theology. I thought if I read the systematic theologies and the books on prayer, then I would love God more. I entered my first church thinking I was mature, because I knew more than the congregants who had been there for years—faithfully attending, serving, and loving. Soon, I realized that as much as I knew, I did not know how to love. The City of Big Brains lured me in unsuspectingly. I thought my head knowledge determined my maturity.

How about you? How have you been shaped by the College for Thinkers? Where have you bought into the idea that your worth is in direct proportion to the grades you get? What temptations do you meet with in pursuing mastery? Where does pride sneak up on you?

Discussion Questions

1. Describe the "aesthetic" of your high school classroom. What did it look like? How were the chairs arranged? What were "desks" like? Which way were they facing? How does the arrangement of the classroom speak to the values and purposes of education?

2. Now, describe the "aesthetic" of your college classroom. In which ways are they alike? In which ways are they dissimilar? How may those similarities and dissimilarities communicate values about education?

3. How have you seen anti-intellectualism or a shallowness infect Christianity and the church? How so? What do you think the solution is?

4. Take a look at the concluding questions above that end the chapter. How do you think you've been influenced by The City of Big Brains? How have you seen this in your K-12 education? How have your goals of education been shaped by the primacy of the mind?

Notes

1. Charles Dickens, *Hard Times*, (New York: Penguin Classics, 2013), 3.

2. As termed in James KA Smith, *Desiring the Kingdom* (Grand Rapids: Baker Academic, 2009), 32.

3. Immanuel Kant, *Kant's Political Writings*, 2nd ed., ed. Hans Reiss (New York: Cambridge University Press, 1991), 54.

4. This phrase referring to "scientism" is attributed to Irving Kristol by David Brooks in *The Social Animal* (New York: Random House, 2012), 226.

5. Perry Glanzer and Todd Ream, *The Idea of a Christian College: A Reexamination for Today's University* (Eugene, OR: Cascade, 2013), 112.

6. Mark Noll, *The Scandal of the Evangelical Mind* (Grand Rapids: W. B. Eerdmans Press, 1994), 3.

7. JP Moreland, *Love Your God with All Your Mind: The Role of Reason in the Life of the Soul* (Colorado Springs: NavPress, 1997), 67.

8. Charles Taylor, "To Follow a Rule," in *Bourdieu: Critical Perspectives*, ed. Craig Calhoun, Edward LiPuma, Moishe Postone (Chicago: University of Chicago Press, 1992), 45-50.

CHAPTER 4

College for Workers:
The City of "Success"

"Education is not primarily an industry, and its proper use is not to serve industries, either by job-training or by industry-subsidized research. Its proper use is to enable citizens to live lives that are economically, politically, socially, and culturally responsible. This cannot be done by gathering or 'assessing' what we now call 'information'—which is to say facts without context and therefore without priority. A proper education enables young people to put their lives in order, which means knowing what things are more important than other things; it means putting first things first."

Wendell Berry, *Thoughts in the Presence of Fear*

There is an old children's story called *The Little Prince* by the French writer Antoine de Saint-Exupéry. It's a beautifully moving picture about life in our modern age. In the film version, there is a young girl with a mom seeking to get into the best school in town: Werth Academy. Her mom has every second of her day scheduled to optimize her potential. The mother desires the best for her little girl—which means full "success" in the workforce. Of course, this is achieved by efficiency, skill, and hardwork—by a true self-made woman. When the girl asks her mom when she can play with a friend, she gives her 30 minutes next Tuesday afternoon. There is not time for leisure or play in our work-a-day world. Success, or being "essential," means going to the best schools so you can have the best job to live in the best neighborhood, and the cycle continues for your child. If all we have is this life, if eternity does not exist, then we need to find our meaning and fulfillment in the here and now. #YOLO, as the kids say.

The Little Prince is a magnificent portrayal of the economic emphasis of our culture. In this analogy, the serious adult world aspires to repress the ancient, child-like world of wonder and enchantment. Success can be attained in this world. It must be. There is no higher power or reality other than your consumer choices. What is important, as the movie depicts, is to "be essential." All that matters is your usefulness. In essence, you go to school to get a good job, because if you get a good job, you will have a nice salary. And a nice salary means you can buy a nice house or car that will attract a nice spouse, so you can parent nice kids and retire to spend all that money you worked so hard for. The purpose of your life is to make money and spend money.

In other words, you are a slave to money and then you die.

The Shaping of the College for Workers

In the last chapter, we looked at the specialization and fragmentation of knowledge that governed academic institutions in the United States before the twentieth century. We saw the fruit (and thorns) of those consequences in the modern education system. "Disciplinary specialization" became the ideal type that fragmented knowledge for the "pure scientist"— specialization has now taken over all subjects. The goal of even literature or philosophy has been shaped by specialization. Instead of seeing the collegiate curriculum as a whole and coherent system, we allowed the curriculum to become divided into specialized units. With a turn to the practical, specialization is no longer about knowledge of a certain area but about qualification for job skills. Here's the move that happens after fragmentation, which this chapter will explain: as education is siphoned off from a holistic goal and internal coherence, it becomes about specialized professions. The goal for students is not about developing as a human beings, but getting whatever the market or the economy demands. In this current conception, if a class does not have immediate skills to make you more employable, what's the point?

With the loss of the authority of religion and older traditions came the rise of the authority of reason. But with first religion rejected and then reason, what matters now is simply what works—what's pragmatic. Presently, college life is largely meant to train students to be educated for "real life," which means they are to be made productive citizens equipped with job skills. The academic endeavor shifted from forming souls as image bearers of God to training employees. With the loss of meaning and purpose, what matters most is what works, and particularly, what pays.

I surmised in the previous chapter that much of your education has been based on something like the scene in *Hard Times* by Charles Dickens: a teacher at the front dispensing facts, and you, as a little pitcher, being filled with those facts. Then, you recite all that you have learned, faithfully repeating what you read or what the teacher said. And we wonder why kids are bored in school.

Here's an example of what the College for Workers nowadays looks like in practice. When you came home from school in the past, your parents or guardians likely asked you some version of the question, "What did you learn today?" Because, ideally, that's what you do in school. However, now that you're in college, thinking about your major, here's what people tend to ask: "What are you going to do with that?" Why? Because we have become smitten with what works, what's practical, and what will serve in making money. And if your major is something that doesn't make sense economically (History, English, Art, or Philosophy, for instance), then it doesn't make sense at all.

In an age past, the university provided stories, language, and curriculum that emphasized the "eulogy virtues," as David Brooks refers to them. These are the good and lasting kinds of things people say about someone who dies well. However, with the increasing modernization of higher education, the university limits itself to the "resumé virtues": those skills that make a person marketable.[1] Today, students have no resources to discuss ultimate meaning or purpose because their whole educational formation is aimed at landing the right job and attaining a lucrative paycheck. A recent study conducted by Perry Glanzer, Jonathan Hill, and Jessica Robinson proves this point. The research group included 229 young emerging adults (ages eighteen to twenty-three), and a majority were either directionless toward their future goals or oriented around individual goals like happiness and material acquisitions.[2] I saw a video on Instagram recently where a business guru with lots of money was explaining what makes him so successful. (And thus, how you can also be successful.) He said he never lets his spouse or kids get in the way of his goals (which are happiness and material acquisitions). Now, here's the thing about a spouse and kids: they get in the way of your goals.

They require time and care and love. And they're worth those sacrifices. Every time. To think that individual happiness and material acquisitions are the goal of life will make you a selfish, distorted, and angry individual. The liberal arts provide a sort of buffer to a pragmatic world that seeks only one's own selfish interest.

You Are What You Earn

I want to provide a brief sketch of how we ended up here. There are two main figures that provide some framing language when it comes to the College for Workers in the City of "Success."

The first is the nineteenth-century German philosopher Friedrich Nietzsche. In the following quote, you will see he has some roots in the College for Thinkers. He wanted an education to develop the scientific man. But, as mentioned above, the scientific man becomes the pragmatic man when the curriculum becomes fractured. He writes, "The education of German youth, however, proceeds from precisely this false and unfruitful conception of culture: its goal, viewed in its essence, is not at all the free cultivated man but the scholar, the man of science, and indeed the most speedily employable man of science."[3] In his understanding, human beings are made for action and earning, hence "the employable man" that college is meant to form. Education, therefore, is for a career—even if it is a scientific career.

There is a short jump, then, to the notion that all education is for employability. Nietzsche goes on to argue, "As much knowledge and education as possible—leading to the greatest possible production and demand—leading to the greatest happiness: that's the formula. Here we have utility as the goal and purpose of education, or more precisely gain: the highest possible income."[4] Very clearly, he states the nature of humans, the goal of education, and the truly happy life. You are what you earn. You are educated to be employed. Your happiness is related to your paycheck.

The second character to introduce is Karl Marx. In the last chapter, I argued that in the College for Thinkers, the view of personhood is *homo cogito*—a thinking thing. Here, in the College for Workers, the image of a person is *homo economicus*—an economic or earning thing. The purpose of economy leads directly to the essential nature of man, which, according to Karl Marx, is labor. He wrote, "The whole of what is called world history is nothing but the creation of man by human labor, and the emergence of nature for man; he therefore has the evident and irrefutable proof of his self-creation, of his own origins." [5] In such a sentiment, humanity has no universal goal. Your community or family has no influence on who you become. You have no inherent gifting. Rather, you are what you make yourself. Humanity operates on an economic principle: get the most you can for the least amount.

In *Habits of Heart*, Robert Bellah and other researchers define this attitude toward life as "utilitarian individualism"—that is, the view of oneself as defined by what works for them. [6] For many in the Western world, especially Americans, all decisions filter through this lens. Benjamin Franklin, that American hero, exemplified the working man. He lived the American dream: he was born poor, he became successful through hard work, and he offered practical advice for common sense virtues. [7] Not only was self-improvement possible, but it could also be divorced from the social context. What matters is *you* becoming successful. After all, as Franklin would contend, "God helps those who help themselves." (FYI: that's not in the Bible). Personal ambition becomes the highest good to be pursued—not growth in character or intellectual development. In the College for Workers, the identity shift is made from the soul (as in the Christian Liberal Arts) to the mind (as in the College for Thinkers) to the individual self. "Success" is the destination to which the self is seeking in the City of "Success." And the idea of success is limited to your financial and personal happiness.

Continuing this theme of how money became the main purpose of education, Neil Postman affirms that "the story tells us that we are first and foremost economic creatures and that our sense of worth and purpose is to be found in our capacity to secure material benefits."[8] Oftentimes, this narrative orients our educational philosophy, even in the Christian college. It tells the student exactly what Nietzsche and Marx articulated: aAperson's main value is their economic utility. Your decisions are only to be made based on how they serve you and make you happy, which, of course, means how much money you make, how big your house is, what kind of car you drive, etc.

With pragmatism and utilitarianism as the way of the university, consumerism currently drives the college experience. Administrators explore what the "consumers" (students and parents) want. They provide resources that will market the right demographic: from movie theaters to sports franchises to ski slopes. You are not a soul to be formed but a consumer to be appeased. The nature of the university is a business corporation first and a place to learn second—or at least so it seems. Therefore, you (and perhaps more likely your parents) wonder if you are getting enough "bang" for your "buck." College tuition is the deposit toward a diploma and a paycheck that is owed—not earned. You have probably seen this in college advertising: here's how much a graduate makes with a degree, what job prospects they have, how our school prepares them for a specific line of work. They argue according to the market because in the world, the market is what matters most.

The Dangers in the City of "Success"

I have been critical of this pragmatic purpose of the university, and I want to be fair. Jobs are important. Neither you nor I want you to be living in your parent's basement at the end of these four years. The charge some may have against a liberal arts education is its impracticality. "Sure," you think, "The liberal arts are great. Easy for you to say. But I have bills to pay. This college is expensive, and I need money." Point taken. However, the value of a good education cannot be reduced to success at getting a job if those joining the workforce are miserable in their jobs. A formative education does not merely educate students with a particular set of life skills; it forms the whole student to flourish in all of life. Wealth, power, influence, and a job can be good things. Christians should want to be good people in top industries. However, jobs or money are terrible goals in and of themselves. There's more to life than how much money you make.

But here's the issue when the goal of life is mere job training: the reason for going to college easily morphs into the pursuit of the American dream—a mobile, middle-class lifestyle and a satisfying career that pays well. Just as reason became inflated in the City for Big Brains, so well-paying jobs become inflated in the City of "Success." In the economy, the logic of capitalism defines human flourishing and happiness. You are defined by your capacity for production and consumption.

What if being honest impeded your bottom line, or if treating others well meant that you paid your employees more (and therefore earned less than you could). Sometimes pursuing the moral thing and the best thing for the company puts a person at odds with career advancement or the next bigger paycheck. Or what if a certain job limits the kind of parent you want to be by the demands it makes on your personal life?

With only "success" in mind oriented around material bene-fits and paycheck, you have no resources to think about the person you want to become. You can get a new job, but you cannot get a new name. Character, who you are, is actually the thing that makes life most meaningful and full of purpose. Even through a pragmatic lens, a bad person cannot make a good employee. Or you can be a great employee and a terri-ble spouse or parent. The City of "Success" often fosters peo-ple who want to do great things, but at the expense of being "great-souled" people—as if you can do great things without the time it takes to foster being a great person.

What About Vocation?

Colleges should prepare students for a career, but the word *vocation* has a much richer and more robust meaning than *merely* career. The word *vocation* stems from the Latin *vocare*: to call. It is what life beckons you to do. Many Christian think-ers have defined it in slightly different ways but with a central theme. Martin Luther King Jr. talks about three dimensions of a vocational call: length, breadth, and height.[9] The length is your personal, inward passions. The breadth is an outward concern for others. And the height is your upward responsibility: duty to a higher being. A complete life needs all three. Tim Keller provides a similar take: A vocation is where affinity, ability, and opportunity line up.[10] What needs do you resonate with? What gifts (and limits) do you have? What does the commu-nity affirm or offer you? Answering those three questions will give you a sense of vocation. And, of course, there's the popular quote from Frederick Buechner: vocation is that "place where your great passion meets the world's great need."[11]

As these definitions outline, the goal is not necessarily looking to find some sort of secret deep within but looking outside of yourself into the world and seeing what life is asking of you. What needs are you passionate about meeting? Where does your heart long to bring restoration and healing to broken systems? What industry or sorts of people do you desire to help?

The social psychologist Jonathan Haidt studied people who were happy. He wanted to discover the factors that contribute to a happy life. He found that people approach their work in one of three ways: as a job, a career, or a calling. A job is a means to make money and maybe enjoy hobbies or friendships on the weekend. A career is seen as a pursuit of promotion and prestige. A calling, on the other hand, finds work intrinsically fulfilling as serving a greater good.[12] The happiest people viewed their profession as a calling or vocation. So, shouldn't colleges prepare people for their vocations?

Admittedly, the idea of vocation can be seen as a bit of a privileged conversation. Some of your parents did not have the freedom or space to think about calling in a way that asked what the world or God is calling of them. They needed to provide, so they got a job. Certainly, as early as three or four hundred years ago, you did what your parents did. If your parent was a fisherman, you were a fisherman. If they were the town butcher, you became the butcher. Many in the world today don't have the luxury to ponder such vocational questions. But calling has deep biblical roots. Abraham was called from the foreign land of Ur to be God's chosen instrument. Isaiah was taken to the throne room of God, purged with a coal, and called to be a witness of God to the people of Israel. Paul encountered Christ on the Damascus Road and was called to be an ambassador for Christ. While most of these have ministry implications, calling also extends beyond ministry. Or maybe better put, your job is a ministry. The reformer

Martin Luther appealed to Psalm 147, where it says God "makes peace at the borders" and "fills the earth with the finest wheat" (v. 14).[13] Now, God does not show up and make peace or fill the market with bread. He uses the police force and firefighters and coast guard and farmers and truck drivers and cashiers to do this work. The Psalmist thanks God in doing all of these things, but in many ways, he is thanking God for the various vocations that make living in safety or eating a sandwich possible. With the biblical idea of vocation, your future vocation is doing God's work in the world. In this way, you are ministering to God and neighbor by what you choose to do—whatever that is.

Vocation is also much broader than the narrow vision of "career" or "job training." The tradition of *vocare* encompasses this broader vision: a calling from God to multiple spheres and identities. In these callings, the underlying purpose of a human continues whether or not a job, location, economy, or trend changes. Discovering and developing purpose provides satisfaction in your multiple callings. Perry Glanzer points out that one is called to many "Great Identities" beyond being a student. You are a friend, neighbor, potential future spouse and parent, citizen, and steward of creation.[14] As such, vocation includes career, but it also moves beyond career. A meaningful life is more than a meaningful job.

Conclusion

In a world that tells you that your value stems from your career success, paycheck, or status, the Christian liberal arts tell a different story. A common question for college students is "What do you want to do?" A much better question is "Who do you want to be?" I'm a cheerleader for this personal, virtue-informed question of vocation. It is in this way that people can experience the harmony of their values with their actions. Educating for a vocation provides the principles behind the behavior. Here's how Cornelius Plantinga explains it:

> In any event your college education is meant to prepare you for prime citizenship in the kingdom of God. For four years or so, such preparation is itself a big part of your vocation. Your calling is to prepare for further calling, and to do so in a Christian college community that cares as much about the kind of person you are becoming as what kind of job you will eventually get, and as much about *how* you will do your job as about *which* job you do.[15]

Plantinga emphasizes the main purpose in your college years: becoming a certain kind of person with values and virtues which inspire how you live your life—including what you do as a career but also what kind of spouse you aspire to be, how you care for your neighbors, how you parent your future children. Which job you have is one important aspect of your life, but it is not the *main* purpose of an education. You can be a great employee and make tons of money but still live a miserable life without cultivating the person you are.

In *The Little Prince*, the girl's successful life is interrupted. Her perfectly organized and scheduled seems to be going great until a propeller flies through the side of the Little Girl's house. The culprit is an odd, eccentric, grandfatherly neighbor. It turns out that this neighbor was an aviator and lived a life of adventure. They develop a friendship that sets the Little Girl on a trajectory to re-imagine the world, to sense the wonder of life, and to value human connection over academic or professional achievement. These are some of the ingredients that make up a meaningful life.

I hope this chapter causes you to re-consider your university education in the same way as the elderly grandfather figure in *The Little Prince*. I want to remind you that you are more than what you do or what you earn. The City of "Success" has a lot of appeal. Money talks, after all. But instead of thinking of your college education as preparation for labor or a specific job, what if you imagined it as a preparation for a life of love? The problem with preparing for a specific job is that you may not have it your whole life. But you know what you will have: the power to love, the foundation to be a certain type of person, and the ability to be faithful. College, then, should be about these eulogy virtues. Sure, I hope your resume looks great. But more than that, I hope you develop to be a great-souled person marked by a love of God and your neighbors. Your vocation is one way to love.

Discussion Questions

1. Try to come up with the 5 most famous people in America today. What makes these people famous? What does this tell you about American values? (And perhaps how you have been shaped by them.)
2. If you were to tell your parents, "I'm more concerned with developing my soul than getting a job during college," how do you think they would react?
3. In what ways have you accepted the "American Dream" that you are what you earn? How has this infiltrated the way you view a college education?
4. How would you define "vocation"? To what different vocations are you called? How do you think college can prepare you for your various vocations?

Notes

1. For the discussion of resume and eulogy virtues, see David Brooks, *The Road to Character* (New York: Random House Trade, 2016).

2. Perry Glanzer, Jonathan Hill, and Jessica Robinson, "Emerging Adult's Conception of Purpose and the Good Life: A Classification and Comparison," *Youth & Society* (2015): 1-19.

3. Friedrich Nietzsche, "On the Use and Abuse of History for Life," trans. Ian C. Johnston, UT Liberal Arts PDF. accessed September 8, 2018, http://la.utexas.edu/users/hcleaver/330T/ 350kPEENietzscheAbuseTableAll.pdf, 42.

4. Friedrich Nietzsche, *Anti-Education: On the Future of Our Educational Institutions*, ed. Paul Rietter and Chad Wellmon (New York: New York Review of Books, 2016).

5. Karl Marx, *Marx's Concept of Man: Including 'Economic and Philosophical Manuscripts'* (London: Bloomsbury, 2014), 139.

6. Robert Bellah et al., *Habits of the Heart: Individualism and Commitment in American Life* (Berkeley: University of California Press, 1985), 32-33.

7. These virtues are recorded in Benjamin Franklin, *Poor Richard's Almanac* (Mineola, NY: Dover Thrift, 1999).

8. Neil Postman, *The End of Education: Redefining the Value of School* (New York: Knopf), 4.

9. Martin Luther King, Jr., "Three Dimensions of a Complete Life," sermon at Dexter Avenue Baptist Church. *Stanford University:* https:// kinginstitute.stanford.edu/king-papers/documents/dimensions-complete-life-sermon-dexter-avenue-baptist-church.

10. Timothy Keller, "Vocation: Discerning Your Calling." *Redeemer City to City.* http://storage.cloversites.com/highpeakfellowship/documents/Vocation-Discerning_Your_Calling.pdf.

11. Frederick Buechner, *Wishful Thinking: A Seeker's ABC* (San Francisco: Harper, 2004), 95.

12. See Jonathan Haidt, *The Happiness Hypothesis: Finding Modern Truth in Ancient Wisdom* (New York: Basic Books, 2006), 221.

13. *Exposition of Psalm 147*, quoted by Gustaf Wingren, *Luther on Vocation* (Evansville, IN: Ballast Press, 1994), 138.

14. Perry Glanzer, "Moving beyond Value or Virtue Added: Transforming Colleges and Universities for Redemptive Moral Development," *Christian Scholar's Review* 39, no. 4 (2010): 379-400.

15. Cornelius Plantinga, *Engaging God's World: A Christian Vision of Faith, Learning, and Living* (Grand Rapids: William B. Eerdmans, 2002), 115.

CHAPTER 5

College for Critics:
The City of Authenticity

"But you cannot go on 'explaining away' forever: you will find that you have explained explanation itself away. You cannot go on 'seeing through' things forever. The whole point of seeing through something is to see something through it. It is good that the window should be transparent, because the street or garden beyond it is opaque. How if you saw through the garden too? It is no use trying to 'see through' first principles. If you see through everything, then everything is transparent. But a wholly transparent world is an invisible world. To 'see through' all things is the same as not to see."

CS Lewis, *The Abolition of Man*

"You do you."
"Follow your heart."
"Be authentic."
"Live your truth."

When you scroll through Instagram, TikTok, or your social media of choice, you will probably come across some of these inspirational phrases. They seem so obvious. Who could challenge their truth?

These ideas are prevalent in our cultural language and art. On Facebook, people share what's "on their hearts" and are praised for their boldness in expressing their authentic selves. In Disney movies, characters overcome a series of challenges to pave a new path forward. In *Moana*, the lead character by the same name could play along with the authorities on the island, but there is something deep inside her more real: her true self which wants to transcend those traditional boundaries. She sings a different song that is wrong to those around her, but maybe hers is the right song.

In many ways, this call to live authentically is good and correct. Moana discovered that her people had a deeper tradition of being wayfarers and not mere island dwellers. By leaving home, she discovered her true self. However, in the modern imagination, tradition has come to be seen as always limiting and mostly harmful.

In our culture these days, authenticity is "the notion that each of us has an original way of being human" and that "each of us has to discover what it is to be ourselves."[1] As such, the way to be human entails originality and precludes convention, authority, and tradition. If someone or some authority says "no" to you, then they're obviously trying to squash your individuality and expression—your very self. Rather than anything we have in common as humans, what becomes most important is how different and unique we are.

However, this authenticity movement breeds a kind of narcissism. "Follow your heart" assumes that whatever is in your heart is good. I don't know about you, but I've got some issues in this heart of mine. But if authentic living means I get to decide what is right and wrong, then whatever someone else says restricts me—maybe even oppresses me. It assumes that I am never wrong and can never be challenged. Anyone who challenges me is a hater. And you know what you do to haters? Block 'em.

But what if self-fulfillment requires unconditional relationships and moral demands? What if growth requires that you leave the echo-chamber of your own heart? What if you need "the haters" to grow?

The Shaping of the College for Critics

Authenticity is rooted in the rise of individualism. Rather than religion or reason, in many ways, the self becomes an idol. And when the self is an idol and supremely important, then no one can or should challenge me. One can see the natural development from "what works for the economy" in the College for Workers to "what works for me" in the College for Critics. When faith and reason lose authority, feelings gain prominence. In a previous age, the individual self is something you needed to overcome. Today, the self is something that needs to be affirmed no matter what.

The goals in the City of "Success" shape the goals in the City of Authenticity. If the main focus of a college is making the consumer (student) happy, then teachers and administrators will do anything to appease them. I can feel the pressure to pass a student despite their effort or even attendance. I want them to be satisfied! Maybe a student will complain about me to my boss! So, perhaps I should not cause students to experience the struggle of a failing grade. The temptation today—even for me as a professor—is to make everybody happy. After all, isn't the Christian college supposed to be a place of grace?

In previous ages, students went outside themselves to discover who they were. Traditional societies arranged their lives around some external reality—whether that is a divine being, science, or the economy. There are inherited norms, commitments, and communities that are helpful to discovering the self. The liberal arts were to remind students what we have in common with each other across age, place, and race as human beings. Today, however, people turn inward. Now, the only source with which to connect is deep inside you. In essence, I determine meaning, purpose, values, and identity. No one else can tell me anything. There is no higher end or purpose to which the self conforms anymore. The only goal is to feel good.

In a study of American culture, a group of researchers led by Robert Bellah investigated what people valued. This is what they found:

> The right act is simply the one that yields the agent the most exciting challenge or the most good feeling about himself. Now if selves are defined by their preferences, but those preferences are arbitrary, then each self constitutes its own moral universe, and there is finally no way to reconcile conflicting claims about what is good in itself. . .All we can appeal to in relationships with others is their self-interest, likewise enlightened, or their intuitive sympathies. . .In the absence of any objectifiable criteria of right and wrong, good or evil, the self and its feelings become our only moral guide.[2]

For those living with this kind of worldview, there is no higher purpose or values to give your life to you. Your feelings are your most true self and must be followed. The only person you can trust is you.

In the College for Workers, we described the view of personhood as being a "utilitarian individualist." In the College for Critics, the group of researchers following Bellah describe the ideal person as an "expressive individualist." In other words, the individual is central, and what gives meaning and purpose in life is the breadth and depth of expression. "Do what feels good," is the mantra. In this culture, the poet Walt Whitman exemplifies the spirit of the age. Rather than a cold, utilitarian ethos, what defines Whitman is "a life rich in experience, open to all kinds of people, luxuriating in the sensual as well as the intellectual, above all a life of strong feeling."[3] This emotivism defines the successful, happy life. Freedom lies in the ability to express oneself.

In *The Malaise of Modernity*, Charles Taylor describes this identity as fragile, needing constant affirmation, and requiring more recognition and support from popular opinion.[4] With a growing regularity, these exact descriptions can chronicle the ethos present on today's college campus. Browse Instagram, and you'll find a plethora of "influencers"—who or what are they influencing? No one really knows. But most profiles I stumble across are desperate attempts to curate one's own "brand"—whatever that brand may be. Flip through a few TikToks, and you'll see clip after clip of those searching for affirmation and likes. Rather than a quest for the good life, what matters is curating one's own lifestyle. Everyone is a winner, and no one is wrong.

Educators came to adopt the "prominence of feelings" paradigm most clearly during the 1960s. During this time, psychologists shaped policy, educational programs, and philosophy.[5] Though many psychologists trained under cognitive and rational philosophies, the application into teaching often focused on the emotions. In short, they believed that personhood functions on the ultimate value of self-esteem. Bettie Youngs articulates the popular sentiment of the day:

> The level of a student's self-esteem is central to school reform, change agency, foreign competition, and just making sure kids turn out as we know they should...

> self-esteem is central to what we make of our lives...It
> is intricately tied to what we will achieve in the course
> of a lifetime. Perhaps nothing affects one's health and
> energy quite so much as the health of our self-es-
> teem. We must not underestimate the role of self-es-
> teem and its contribution to student achievement and
> performance...Positive self-esteem is essential for all
> youngsters if they are to develop in healthy ways.[6]

Essentially, in this understanding, teaching should soothe
self-esteem. Feelings become sacred. As long as people are
feeling good and undergo no duress, students will be happy and successful. Right and wrong is determined by how it
makes you feel.

This focus on emotional fragility presents itself in the
Christian tradition as well. For example, in one mainline de-
nomination, a pamphlet describes the beginning and center of
the moral life as self-understanding and self-love ("self-understanding, self-worth, self-acceptance, self-image, or just feeling
good about yourself").[7] Emotions become the guide to truth
and to reality in numerous ways. The self becomes the sacred.

With this particular philosophical foundation, the modern
campus does not have the resources to discuss personal weakness; there are merely differences. The great men and women
of the past needed to be challenged, offended, and suffer to
overcome life's challenges. As much as I wish it were different,
pain builds character and strengthens a person's weakness. In
a *New York Times* article, Judith Schulevitz describes how colleges should encourage challenging topics and ideas. She writes,

> Shield them from unfamiliar ideas and they'll never
> learn the discipline of seeing the world as other people
> see it. They'll be unprepared for the social and intellec-
> tual headwinds that will hit them as soon as they step

off the campuses whose climates they have so carefully controlled. What will they do when they hear opinions they've learned to shrink from? If they want to change the world, how will they learn to persuade people to join them? [8]

In previous ages, education was transformative. In the City of Authenticity, the purpose of education is therapeutic. Perhaps more than any other City, there are no longer standards or norms to instruct life or education. If someone can define their identity, they can also define the goal of education for themselves. The only expectation is fulfillment and satisfaction. The ideals of education are internal to the self. Niceness is the supreme virtue. To challenge someone else's truth claim is cruel and disagreeing becomes harmful to the self.

A Few Disclaimers

Let me clear up a few things. First, I am not some sort of masochist who wants to cause pain in the classroom. I am not out to cause undue harm. But the task of education is stretching because growing is painful. If you leave college thinking the exact same things that you believe today, either college has failed you, or you have failed yourself. The university is meant to unsettle you. The examined life is uncomfortable. Personally, I'd rather just think I'm right and not be challenged. I don't want to consider that I may be wrong about something.

Jonathan Haidt wrote a piercing article in *The Atlantic* entitled, "The Coddling of the American Mind." He asserts:

Emotional reasoning dominates many campus debates and discussions. A claim that someone's words are 'offensive' is not just an expression of one's own subjective feeling of offendedness. It is, rather, a public charge that the speaker has done something objectively wrong. It is

> a demand that the speaker apologize or be punished by
> some authority for committing an offense.[9]

In the modern university culture that Haidt so accurately
describes, "I'm offended" becomes the unbeatable trump card.
All reasonable, respectable discussion and dialogue comes to
a halt. Offensiveness is the unpardonable sin—worthy to be
canceled over.

You can see this in conservative circles as well as liberal
ones. In today's most controversial news, "critical race theory"
has become some sort of heresy that cannot be discussed. If
you are on a conservative campus, to listen to someone identified with critical race theory comes with the threat of "can-
cellation." Likewise, on the left, if someone finds out that you
listen to a conservative podcast—whether you agree with
them or not—you are a supporter of the patriarchy. In some
places, nuance and empathy are nearly gone. Too often, guilt
by association reigns.

By no means am I seeking to be offensive or provoke my
students for the sake of provocation. There are some who have
become famous for being jerks. I try to not be a jerk (at least I
hope). However, having hard conversations is…hard. It comes
with the risk of offense or causing pain. Stewarding my authority as a professor may mean guiding conversations into complicated territory, but a wise leader does not "coddle" for the sake
of non-offense. It would be like a coach never pushing you to
weight train, because your muscles will hurt. Sometimes, pain
is where the growth is. In my best, most engaged classes, students (I hope!) will disagree with one another. They will disagree with me! But they will be challenged to articulate their
case for a given stance and be sharpened in the process.

Second, and undeniably, emotions are powerful. David
Hume asserts, "Reason is, and ought only to be the slave

of the passions, and can never pretend to any other office than to serve and obey them."[10] In many ways, Hume is exactly right: emotions often dictate how humanity reasons. Emotions are the expression of desire. My critique is not to ignore feelings, but to place feelings in their proper place. The pastor and theologian Jonathan Edwards urges, "The right way, is not to reject all affections, nor to approve all; but to distinguish affections, approving some, and rejecting others; separating between the wheat and the chaff, the gold and the dross, the precious and the vile."[11] True religion consists of correct religious affections that influence the will of the soul. Knowers have biases and emotional predispositions. Humans cannot carry a purely cognitive load. Alan Jacobs urges that "learning to feel as we should is enormously helpful for learning to think as we should."[12] Experience matters, but my experience does not determine the truth. I could feel like a person disrespected me by not responding to me when I spoke. However, he or she may not have heard me. Or you may feel like you bombed a test. But you may get it back and find out you did great. Your experience is important, but it should not dictate reality.

The Dangers in the City of Authenticity

I have discussed the rise of feelings and emotions in recent history, but what does that have to do with critique? Why have I called this the "College for Critics?"

One of the main philosophical influences in the understanding of self and truth is Michel Foucault. One of his main contributions to academia is the teaching that all truth claims are assertions to power. In other words, he believed that when I say something is true, the reason I want it to be true is that it gives me power over you. He argues,

> Truth is a thing of this world: it is produced only by virtue
> of multiple forms of constraint. And it induces regular
> effects of power. Each society has its regime of truth, its
> "general politics" of truth: that is, the types of discourse
> which it accepts and makes function as true; the mech-
> anisms and instances which enable one to distinguish
> true and false statements, the means by which each is
> sanctioned; the techniques and procedures accorded
> value in the acquisition of truth; the status of those who
> are charged with saying what counts as true.[13]

Notice that first sentence: truth is a thing of this world. Truth,
so conceived, is a product of our environment or social circumstance. Foucault is arguing that there are no universal
truths that are true for all people. Truth is what I determine.
And I want my truth to be true to coerce you to my way of
being. As a white, straight, Christian male, I have the most
power, so obviously, I am advocating my truth to oppress you,
because I have power to lose if you are right.

So, let's say you correct me in class. Even if I admit you
are right, I lose authority in the classroom. Rather than say
I'm wrong, it's natural for me to argue my point and prove my
authority. It's the way power works. You need to stay in your
place.

Now, to be fair and charitable, there is an aspect of truth
that Foucault and others in his postmodern school of thought
gets. All truth claims are cultural creations. I cannot avoid that.
At its simplest level, I am writing (and you are reading) in English. That is a cultural creation. I am writing as a white male,
which means I write from a certain sociological understanding.
Foucault raises a good question: Why do I believe what I do?
And how does having power inform my truth claims?

But if I define truth by myself, since I am the center of
determining truth, then when you attack truth, you are

attacking me—my authentic self. Herein lies the main issue with self-dictating truth: a discussion of truth becomes a discussion of the self. When someone attacks this idea that I hold, they are attacking me, or so the theory goes. Any attempt to persuade, no matter how patiently or kindly, is an attempt to dominate and proselytize. Difference of opinion becomes war. This way of imagining truth and education deconstructs the task of education. Believe it or not, this is one of the major trends among those who study higher education these days.

In a recent article titled "The Age of Outrage," Jonathan Haidt describes the phenomenon:

> Everything is about power. Every situation is to be analyzed in terms of the bad people acting to preserve their power and privilege over the good people. This is not an education. This is induction into a cult, a fundamentalist religion, a paranoid worldview that separates people from each other and sends them down the road to alienation, anxiety, and intellectual impotence.[14]

In many ways, the title of his article is fitting: the City of Authenticity quickly descends into an age of outrage. In some of today's college environments, to even understand a viewpoint you disagree with makes you an accomplice to oppression.

My fear is that we will never learn to appreciate other perspectives if all we do is critique. If every truth claim is a power claim and the only authority to discern power and oppression is the self, then I myself am the arbitrator of all truth. And in my truth seeking, I am constantly reading between the lines attempting to see how someone is using their power to try to "get" or oppress me. My posture becomes one of critique where I am always looking to tear down but never to build up. To be clear, critique is not always bad, but it has some limitations. It is necessary to offer critique, but when being

critical is all we learn how to do, then we never get around to
constructing something beautiful.

Rather than only critique, I want to suggest a way of
learning that includes what I call contemplation. When you
hear someone say something you disagree with, give it a moment. Think deeply. Reflect. Like contemplation, it will take
some time, and there will be very few easy answers.

In an episode of *Ted Lasso*, Ted, the coach of fictional AFC
Richmond, is playing darts in a competition with the former
owner, Rupert. They make a bet: if Rupert wins, he gets to pick
the starting lineup for the last two (consequential) games. If
Ted wins, Rupert can't go anywhere near the owner's box. Ted
is down to three darts, and he needs two triple twenties and
a bullseye to win. Things are looking bleak. He goes into a
monologue about how people have always underestimated
him. About how on the way to school one day, he saw a quote
by Walt Whitman that said, "Be curious, not judgmental."[15]
Ted hits his first triple twenty. He realizes that all "them fel-
las" that used to belittle him weren't curious. They thought they
had everything figured out, and so they judged everyone and
everything. If they were curious, they would have asked questions like, "Have you played a lot of darts, Ted?" At this point,
he nails his second triple twenty. And you can see where this is
going. Ted goes on to win and defends his new friend, so that
Rupert can't sit in the owner's box next to her. It may be the best
clip of television in recent history.

With this Lassoian wisdom, let's not be afraid to ask questions. Why do they believe that? What sources of truth are
they appealing to? Why would someone find that truth compelling? In other words, do not start with critique. To always
start with critique, you are assuming that you are right and
now your job is to tell someone how wrong they are. Last
time I checked, that convinced exactly zero people of the

truth. Rather, assume some humility—maybe they possess something worth believing. Be respectful of another person made in the image of God. You may well be right on a subject. But before you launch into critique, spend some time to understand. Pause and contemplate.

Conclusion

As I have taught students over the years, I think this idea of critique is the atmosphere you may "feel" the most. This is the sense of your world today. Rather than speak about a controversial issue, you stay silent in fear of being ridiculed or getting canceled for saying something "offensive." This type of college atmosphere stifles vibrant education. In my classes, when we discuss race, gender, or any other controversial issue, rather than speaking honestly and seeking to understand, typically the class atmosphere is one of silence. We'd rather keep our thoughts to ourselves lest we risk making ourselves or someone else uncomfortable. But what if a good education is at odds with the comfort of so-called authenticity?

The philosopher Alasdair MacIntyre is worth quoting at length as he describes the ideal college setting:

> The university [should become] a place of constrained disagreement, of imposed participation in conflict, in which a central responsibility of higher education would be to initiate students into conflict. In such a university those engaged in teaching and enquiry would have to play a double role...The first of these would be to advance enquiry from within that particular point of view, preserving and transforming the initial agreements with those who share that point of view...The second task would be to enter into contro-

versy with other rival standpoints, doing so both in order to exhibit what is mistaken in that rival standpoint
in the light of the understanding afforded by one's
own point of view and in order to test and retest the
central theses advanced from ones' own point of view
against the strongest possible objections to them to be
derived from one's opponents...[The reason for this is] to
ensure that rival voices were not illegitimately suppressed, to sustain the university—not as an arena of
neutral objectivity, as in the liberal university, since
each of the contending standpoints would be advanc-
ing its own partisan account of the nature and function
of objectivity—but as an arena of conflict in which the
most fundamental type of moral and theological disagreement was accorded recognition.[16]

The best way to pursue a college education is to engage in robust
discussions about truth. First, understand your side of the argument with the best of the thinkers from your position. Then,
spend the same amount of time and effort to understand someone else's position considering the best thinkers and arguments.
The college campus is a unique setting where this exchange of
ideas can happen—and colleges need to let this process happen.
To silence a voice is oppressive. But the college functions as an
arena of conflict where we are sharpened for clearer and better
thinking. Particularly as a Christian college, we have the resources to display civil discourse better than anyone. We have
Christ and his gospel in common, so we can exhibit grace to
discuss all sorts of other disagreements.

To be sure, sometimes systems of thought are oppressive.
Some ideas are plays at power that need to be torn down.
Some tradition needs to be rejected. But you also need the
resources to build something in its place. So, what would a

new vision of a Christian liberal arts college look like? What would an education look like that pursued love? In other words, what am I proposing that is different than the models that I have outlined and critiqued? I'm glad you asked. In the following chapter, I will lay out my vision for an education worth pursuing.

Discussion Questions

1. Are there any subjects that you feel are "off-limits" lest you be "canceled?" What are they? Why?
2. Describe a time when you did not speak up about something for fear you would say something offensive or ignorant.
3. What are the problems with an overemphasis of "self-esteem"?
4. Typically, people respond in two ways to conflict: fight or flight. Are you more prone to shut down when conflict occurs or fight? Why do you think that is? Describe a time when your response got you in trouble.

Notes

1. Charles Taylor, *Ethics of Authenticity* (Cambridge, MA: Harvard University Press, 1992), 61.

2. Robert Bellah, et al., *Habits of the Heart: Individualism and Commitment in American Life* (Berkeley: University of California Press, 1985), 76.

3. Ibid., 34.

4. Charles Taylor, *The Malaise of Modernity* (Toronto: House of Anansi Press, 2003).

5. James Davison Hunter, *Death of Character: Moral Education in An Age Without Good or Evil* (New York: Basic Books, 2001), 81-106. Hunter outlines the history and gives examples of expressivist strands of moral education, sex education, parenting literature, and drug education with the goal of building self-esteem.

6. Bettie B. Youngs, "Self-Esteem in the School," *NASSP Bulletin* (January 1993): 59, 59-60, 65-66.

7. Herman C. Ahrens, *Feeling Good about Yourself: Helping Young People Build Self-Esteem* (New York: Pilgrim Press, 1983), 3.

8. Judith Shulevitz, "In College and Hiding from Scary Ideas," *The New York Times*, March 21, 2015, https://www.nytimes.com/2015/03/22/opinion/sunday/judith-shulevitz-hiding-from-scary-ideas.html).

9. Jonathan Haidt and Greg Lukianoff, "The Coddling of the American Mind," *The Atlantic*, September 2015, https://www.theatlantic.com/magazine/archive/2015/09/the-coddling-of-the-american-mind/399356/.

10. David Hume, *A Treatise of Human Nature* (Charleston, SC: Createspace, 2016), 462.

11. Jonathan Edwards, "The Nature of True Virtue," in *The Works of Jonathan Edwards,* ed. Henry Rogers and Edward Hickman (Peabody, MA: Hendrickson, 2005), 121.

12. Alan Jacobs, *How to Think: A Survival Guide for a World at Odds* (New York: Currency, 2017), 87.

13. Michel Foucault, *The Foucault Reader,* ed. Paul Rabinow (New York: Pantheon, 1984), 199.

14. Jonathan Haidt, "The Age of Outrage," Wriston Lecture for the Manhattan Institute, November 15, 2017, https://www.city-journal.org/html/age-outrage-15608.html.

15. *Ted Lasso*, Season 1, Episode 8, "The Diamond Dogs," Directed by Declan Lowney, written by Leann Bowen, aired September 18, 2020, on Apple TV, https://tv.apple.com/us/episode/the-diamond-dogs/umc.cmc.eaaizh8wdtnjuohaebw843ft?showId=umc.cmc.vtoh0mn0x-n7t3c643xqonfzy.

16. Alasdair MacIntyre, *Three Rival Versions of Moral Enquiry: Encyclopaedia, Genealogy, and Tradition: Being Gifford Lectures Delivered in the University of Edinburgh in 1988* (Notre Dame: University of Notre Dame Press, 2014), 230-31.

CHAPTER 6

College is for Lovers: The Pilgrim's Foundation for the Journey

"Some seek knowledge for
The sake of knowledge:
That is curiosity;
Others seek knowledge so that
They themselves may be known:
That is vanity;
But there are still others
Who seek knowledge in
Order to serve and edify others:
And that is charity."

Bernard of Clairvaux, *Selected Works*

There is something wonderful about commencement addresses. You come to the end of an academic career, sitting with close friends, surrounded by family, reflecting on memories, excited about the future. To be fair, I don't remember any of the commencement addresses when I was graduating, but maybe you will. I wanted to be done, get my diploma, and get going. However, I do enjoy listening to commencement addresses from other graduation ceremonies. (Is that weird?)

Right around early May each year, you can expect to find a few noteworthy commencement examples pop across your social media feed. Equal parts challenging and inspiring, the best ones cut through superficial concerns and go straight to the heart of why you spend four years in an academic institution. What were those four years about anyway? What was I supposed to get from them? These speeches are a way to reflect, evaluate, and look forward on a momentous day. Or at least they should.

David Foster Wallace offered one of the most famous commencement speeches in recent history. Wallace was a novelist by training and was regarded by many as one of the leading writers of his day. He strolled onto the campus of Kenyon College in the springtime of 2005 and walked up to the lectern. Serious yet humorous, he described the value of a liberal arts education as teaching us not only how to think (that famous liberal arts cliché) but what to think *about*. He began with a quippy story about fish in water. An old fish passes two young fish and says, "Hey boys. How's the water?" The two young fish then turn to one another and ask, "What the hell is water?"

Wallace uses this introduction to beckon the graduating students to consider their default positions: What do you think is normal? Why are things the way they are? What don't you even think about doubting? Some things seem so obvious that they're hard to notice—like fish in water. Perhaps you've never doubted that God exists or that He's good. College is a time to wrestle and engage with your default position. Why do you believe that? Can you be sure? How? Maybe you are the opposite: of course, God doesn't exist. Nobody can prove he does. You're a scientific person.

College is a time to doubt your doubts—to really investigate the water we are all swimming in—whether that's American culture, Christian culture, or college culture. These previous chapters were a way to get on dry land and evaluate the water. What kind of water have you been swimming in that you haven't noticed?

One of the most pressing realities that Wallace brought to the surface is this—everyone assumes that they are the absolute center of the universe and that the world revolves around them. Consider this reality for a moment: every experience happens to you. People annoy you or bother you or slow you down. You aren't the problem—you are the way you are. Others are the ones that need to change. Why? Because you are obviously right, good, and true. Other people are the issue. Since this posture tends to be our default position, he suggests that "learning how to think really means learning how to exercise some control over how and what you think. It means being conscious and aware enough to choose what you pay attention to and to choose how you construct meaning from experience. Because if you cannot exercise this kind of choice in adult life, you will be totally hosed."[1] If you never question the water you swim in, there's a good chance you'll swim along pursuing a successful, comfortable, upwardly mobile American life, which most people just take for granted. The American dream includes going to college to be smart and being smart means getting a good degree which will make good money. If you do that, you will be happy, or so we assume. It's the air we breathe, the water in which we swim. Now, these are fine things to pursue, but if you never question this water of the assumed good life, as Wallace suggests, you will be totally hosed. Part of the next four years is taking a meta-look at your consciousness and awareness—thinking about your thinking.

How will you decide what has value and what doesn't? How will you decide how to interpret mundane events like losing your keys, sitting in traffic, or waiting in line? What's the point of suffering? In essence, Wallace asks, what and how will you decide to worship? He continues:

> Because here's something else that's weird but true: in the day-to-day trenches of adult life, there is actually no such thing as atheism. There is no such thing as not worshipping. Everybody worships. The only choice we get is what to worship. And the compelling reason for maybe choosing some sort of god or spiritual-type thing to worship–be it JC or Allah, be it YHWH or the Wiccan Mother Goddess, or the Four Noble Truths, or some inviolable set of ethical principles–is that pretty much anything else you worship will eat you alive. If you worship money and things, if they are where you tap real meaning in life, then you will never have enough, never feel you have enough. It's the truth. Worship your body and beauty and sexual allure and you will always feel ugly. And when time and age start showing, you will die a million deaths before they finally grieve you. On one level, we all know this stuff already. It's been codified as myths, proverbs, clichés, epigrams, parables; the skeleton of every great story. The whole trick is keeping the truth up front in daily consciousness.

> Worship power, you will end up feeling weak and afraid, and you will need ever more power over others to numb you to your own fear. Worship your intellect, being seen as smart, you will end up feeling stupid, a fraud, always on the verge of being found out. But the insidious thing about these forms of worship is not that they're evil or sinful, it's that they're unconscious. They are default settings. They're the kind of worship you just gradually slip into,

day after day, getting more and more selective about what you see and how you measure value without ever being fully aware that that's what you're doing.[2]

Wallace never identified as a Christian, but he sees something central to human reality: everyone worships. Something always rules the heart. And whatever rules the heart provides our interpretive framework of reality. Each of us gets to choose what we worship. How will you decide?

Education as Worship

We are a "god-making species" or as a reformed theologian John Calvin is oft quoted, our hearts are "perpetual idol-making factories."[3] We tell stories that make sense of our various gods. The previous chapters were stories of others who make gods and seduce us by making a *good* thing into an *ultimate* thing. Each "City" made sense of the world by assigning ultimate meaning to some feature of existence. Each of the chapters explored those who took a good narrative and made it ultimate; in a real sense, these thinkers made one aspect of the educational task a "god." For example, the College for Thinkers made the mind a "god"—this aspect became the orientating principle to which everything needs to submit. The College for Workers made employment a god—a good outcome taken to an ungodly importance. The College for Critics made the self a god. While each chapter introduced us to influential leaders who added something unique to the educational task, taken to the extreme—to god-like status—these aspects all become disordered. Each of the previous educational philosophies asked important questions that are necessary but provided insufficient answers. In other words, each of the previous educational philosophies is needed but it cannot bear the weight of a holistic and fruitful college education. There must be something more, something deeper, something more central that unifies and holds the limited models together.

The crucial question to consider during college is this: "What do you love *most*?" or in Wallace's words, "What will you worship?" What will be the orientating principle to which your life revolves?

Each Sunday, many churches throughout the world begin their service with "The Summary of the Law." One of the first things Christians hear each week is Jesus' words defining a purposeful life. Here's what he says: "You shall love the Lord your God with all your heart and with all your soul and with all your mind. This is the first and great commandment. And the second is like it: You shall love your neighbor as yourself. On these two commandments depend all the Law and the Prophets" (Matt. 22:37-40). These verses have come to be known as the "Great Commandment." Jesus guides us into our priorities for life: we are to love God and our neighbor.

On this twin command, the ancient African bishop St. Augustine writes, "The aim of the command is love, a twofold love of God and of one's neighbor. But if you understand by this your whole persons—mind and body—and your whole neighbor—that is, his mind and body, for a person consists of mind and body—no class of things to be loved is missing from these two commandments."[4] In other words, all of life and all of one's loves can be included under these two commands—including education. Everything we do involves loving God and loving your neighbor. When you read a book, you are exercising loving attention. When you listen to a fellow student say something silly, you can care by kindly engaging. When you write a paper or respond to a professor, love can and ought to be the motivating principle. The classroom does not operate by some set of alternative priorities.

After "The Summary of the Law," the people pray, "Lord, have mercy." After hearing the standard of life that Jesus invites us into, the only right response is, "Oh, crap." Can any of us consistently hold to these standards? No way. Whenever these twin commands are not followed, restlessness ensues. We were meant to worship God, but we worship created things instead. Thus, one of St. Augustine's most famous lines in the *Confessions* is, "Our souls are restless until they rest in You."[5] If you seek fulfillment or "rest" in your job, you'll always be unhappy because there is always more work to do. If you put your happiness in your intellectual ability, you'll always be disappointed because someone will always be smarter than you or get better grades. This is what David Foster Wallace was saying in his colorful warning when he argued that these wrong priorities will "eat you alive." However, when your love is rightly ordered, there can be harmony and rest, which is the flourishing life. Happiness consists of loving God and loving one's neighbor in God, and this pursuit should be central to your college years. This idea of happiness will surely affect life after college.

More to the point, here's what Augustine argues regarding education:

> Whoever, therefore, thinks that he understands the divine Scriptures or any part of them in such a way that [his interpretation] does not build the double love of God and of our neighbor does not understand [the Scriptures] at all. Whoever finds a lesson there useful to the building of charity, even though he has not said what the author may be shown to have intended in that place, has not been deceived, nor is he lying in any way.[6]

Augustine's application to the divine Scriptures is true for any educational endeavor. If any learning does not build the double love of God and neighbor, it is futile. As you're learning various subjects in the years to come, you ought to be asking, "How can this class increase my love for God?" Or "How could I use this project to serve my neighbor?" Or "How do I think about my vocation in such a way that my job meets the needs of my neighbors in a loving manner?" Or to bring Wallace back to the conversation, "How does the priority of love of God and neighbor change how I pay attention? How does it alter what I am conscious of? What is my default setting, and does it need to change?" Not every class that you take will adequately address these foundational questions, but they are questions you can bring to your education. They are relatively holistic questions—is there anything that cannot be applied to loving God and your neighbor?

Caring About What God Cares About

The priority of love does not neglect the other important questions or issues we discussed in the previous chapters— questions of the nature of knowledge, a meaningful career, or the necessity of loving critique. However, the idea of ordered love does organize these previous priorities and seeks to root those questions in a more robust framework. Baylor professor Alan Jacobs proposes, "Our goal... (is) to love as widely and as well as our limited selves will allow."[7] Jacobs' "widely" applies to every subject, every book, every academic pursuit, and every co-curricular activity. It is the college's best aim to invite students to love widely and well. If you remember, this sentiment is key to how I define an education in the Introduction: ordering and expanding our love.

If we take the love-oriented direction of a Christian liberal arts college, then there's nothing beyond our care.

Think about it. If God made everything and if everything He made was good, then saying "I do not care" basically means saying, "I do not care about God." That seems like a harsh way of saying things, but I think it's true. It's also why I think Christians should be the most interesting and interested people in a room. Taking God's vision, we have the greatest capacity to care. Everyone you encounter, each subject you are learning, is an opportunity to know more (and love more) about the God behind it. Or, at the very least, learning about mundane or "boring" subjects is a way to exercise love for your neighbor who does care about such a subject. I do not care about operas but there are some people who do—and there are good reasons to like operas.

A Christian liberal arts education encourages holistic care. Since you cannot be reduced to a mind, a body, or your feelings, subjects across various disciplines and fields cultivate you in certain ways. To neglect mathematical precision is to be deformed in a particular capacity that God has given you. To think psychology is just for those "feelings people" is to neglect your own emotional development. Even to look down on trades or recreation studies as "the practical or servile arts" is to be inattentive to your body. Holistic formation requires that we care and pursue the broad way in which God created us. We need the liberal arts because we are complex.

This is not a suggestion to neglect career and vocational formation. As much as we need the "liberal" formation, college is also about being specific. You have particular interests, gifts, and passions that need to be cultivated. You will likely pursue some specific course of study. We call it having a "major" or "minor". You need to go deep in one area of interest. But if you neglect holistic formation, then you'll also reduce your capacity to care along the way. You are more than even your interests.

You are What You Worship

How should we think about ourselves as students on the path of learning in love, even through our college studies? If the goal of life (and education) is to love God and your neighbor, what view of personhood fosters a loving posture in learning? Remember Marilynne Robinson's quote in the Introduction: how we view ourselves has everything to do with how we treat one another. If we are not thinking things, material things, or an unencumbered self, then who are we? And how does our view of ourselves lead us to how we treat one another?

Here's where understanding the past chapters is important. If we are just big brains primed for information, then the way we tend to love God is by having more theology or more religious information. This view suggests that to know more is to love more. Your worth is what you know. Or, if we are merely economic beings who live to make money, then we may love and worship God on Sunday, which is well and good, but Monday through Friday are disconnected from that. Worship and work exist in two different realms, and as much as you are told your worth is tied to your identity in Christ, for most of the week, you are being formed in a culture that says your worth is in what you make. An inadequate view of the human person—yourself and others—always leads to a distorted approach to faith.

But in the biblical scheme of things, central to how we understand ourselves is an image bearer of God. Genesis 1:27 reads, "So God created man in his own image, in the image of God he created him; male and female he created them." Much debate has been had and many books have been written on what the "image of God" means. Is it our rational ability that is like God? Is it our relational nature? The promise attached to humanity? Is it the command to take care of the earth and cultivate creation? All good questions and answers. For now, it's important to see the dignity God bestows on humanity. No other created being is in the image of God. There is a unique status God places on men and women. Whether you identify as religious or not is beside the point for now. I think we can all agree there is something about us—some essential part—that does not have a shape or location. We can experience awe and be overwhelmed. We experience love and beauty in a way that distinguishes us from the animal world or inanimate things.

God declares that you and I are sacred—like Himself in a mysterious way. We are not just brains-on-a-stick, computing machines, or effective laborers. We are given worth and status by the one who fashioned us. We are made in God's image. God loves us because He made us, and we are to love others, because God loves them too. We exist as adorers—lovers. Wallace was right: everyone worships something. To desire is human.

To add complexity to our understanding of ourselves, we are also sinners. We have disordered desires. We wrongly worship. We have marred the goodness in which God made us. I think all of us have had the experience of deep shame or regret—of doing or saying something we wish we could take back. (And if you haven't, you will.) "Sin" is the biblical word, but you can call it what you wish. We have blown it. We have loved the wrong things. And because our desires are twisted, we think wrongly and choose wrongly. Our problem runs deep. Summarizing the reformer Thomas Cranmer, Ashley Null writes, "What the heart loves, the will chooses, and the mind justifies. The mind doesn't direct the will. The mind is actually captive to what the will wants, and the will itself, in turn, is captive to what the heart wants."[8] Did you catch that? The heart or desire is central. Even the way we use our reason is subject to what we want. As a basic (and extreme) example, think about World War II and Nazi Germany. At the time, Germany was one of the most advanced countries in the world with the world's best universities. They had all the rational capabilities. However, how did they use their reason? To kill and destroy. Their desire distorted their thinking. They could rationally justify their evil. Perhaps we are not as extreme, but we function the same way. We rationalize what we want.

So here we are—both depraved and dignified, fallen yet redeemable, created good with deep stains, lost with lingering goodness. Our desires are distorted. But what does that have to do with education? This is a book about education, right?

This has everything to do with education. How we view ourselves influences how we will treat one another. We need a vision of education that accounts for all our complexity—as teachers and as students.

The Latin root word where we get education is *educere*, which means to draw out. Part of the college years is to draw out that which is good. As an image bearer, you have essences of goodness and truth inside of you. It's in there for you to find. Finding out who you are is an important task of a college education.

You may have come across Plato's allegory of the cave in your education.[9] Plato was an early Greek philosopher before the time of Jesus. By all accounts, he was one of the most profound thinkers in the history of the world. He developed the thought of his teacher Socrates, who illustrated that human experience is like being prisoners locked in a cave since birth facing a blank wall. There is a fire behind them, and people and things pass behind them that project shadows on the blank wall in front of them. For all their lives, they think the shadow of a puppet elephant is an elephant or the shadow of a cut out hammer is a hammer. All they have known is the shadow. Eventually, one of the prisoners escapes and enters the world lit by the sun. At first, he is blinded. Think about being in the dark your whole life and finally encountering the sun. It would be overwhelming and disorienting. But the purpose of the enlightened is to go back to the cave to help fellow "prisoners"—to show the way to true light and life. The path of education is about developing deeper understanding over shallow answers.

There's so much about Plato's analogy that relates to education, but at the very least, here's what Plato is onto: you have the resources to discover truth. Made in the image of God, every human being does. We have gifts and capacities to see the goodness, truth, and beauty of the world when we study it. All you need is to be released from the cave.

But there is also some chipping away that needs to be done due to our sinful desires. We need some help. Here's where we need the wise guides who have seen the light, who are deep people, to help make us people of depth. You need others to cultivate the gifts you possess. That's where other students and teachers can assist. As much as we've been taught to be independent, we need others. We need their perspective to draw us out of our faulty beliefs or desires, and they may need us to correct their errors. Truth is clarified in community. Education starts with someone who has seen the sun and returns to tell you in the cave.

Image bearer and beloved sinner, our loves need to be drawn out, and they need to be cultivated. You have something to bring to the educational task. Fellow students have broadening perspectives and teachers can be wise guides.

Conclusion

Each human you encounter is a mystery—whether that be the author of a book or the professor lecturing. They come to you with a mix of good and bad, true and false, beautiful and ugly. No matter how disordered, annoying, or wrong, each person is sacred. How you treat others is in a very real sense how you treat God (Matt. 25:40).

As human beings, we are complex souls who shouldn't be reduced to some aspect of our being. Lovers, *homo adorans*: this is who we are. Everyone worships. Love requires thinking, doing, and feeling. But desire drives each one. As an image bearer of God, you have worth because you exist. And there is more to develop in our natural capacity. There is more to life than *mere* existence or shadowy realities. The way we find true meaning or the way we live the good life is through ordering what we love. If we love something good but not ultimate, we will be restless. And here's the secret to our human dilemma: the way to rest is through loving God and your neighbor. If we order our lives according to these priorities, our living—including learning and working—will be fulfilling. A college education, therefore, is not just learning a few facts in four years. Rather, an education worth having is about forming you into a certain type of person. The liberal arts can help us see there is more to love in the world.

So how do we go about these college years in a way that will lead to flourishing in the rest of life? I'm glad you asked. That's what Part Two seeks to answer.

Discussion Questions

1. What do you think about the idea that "everyone worships"—even those who do not believe in some higher power?

2. If you were to spend some time thinking about what you love the most (or what you worship), what do you think it is? (What would make you happy? What do you find the ultimate good? What do you spend most of your time thinking about? If something was taken away, what would be unbearable?)

3. Prioritize a list of ten things you love most in order. What would it look like to live in a way where your life reflects your love? What changes would you need to make?

4. In this chapter, Sosler reminds you of his definition of education: ordering and expanding love. Having read the previous chapters now, evaluate his idea of education. What do you think? What's left out? What's limited? How would you define education?

Notes

1. David Foster Wallace, "This Is Water," Commencement Address at Kenyon College, accessed August 11, 2018, https://web.ics.purdue.edu/~drkelly/DFWKenyonAddress2005.pdf.

2. Ibid.

3. John Calvin, *Institutes of the Christian Religion*, trans. H. Beveridge, (Peabody, MA: Hendrickson, 2008), 59.

4. Augustine, *On Christian Teaching*, trans. R. P. H. Green (New York, NY: Oxford University Press, 1999), 20.

5. Augustine, *Confessions*. ed. and trans. Carolyn Hammond. Loeb Classical Library (Cambridge, MA: Harvard University Press, 2014), 1.

6. Augustine, *On Christian Teaching*, 30.

7. Alan Jacobs, *The Pleasures of Reading in an Age of Distraction* (Oxford: Oxford University Press), 135.

8. See "Dr. Ashley Null on Thomas Cranmer," *Anglican Church League, Sydney, Australia*, (September 2001), http://acl.asn.au/resources/dr-ashley-null-on-thomas-cranmer/.

9. Plato, *Republic*, 514a–520a.

REST STOP

On the pilgrim's journey, sometimes it's helpful to take a break, survey where you've been, and set a vision of where you'll go. So far, each chapter corresponds to a lens with which particular colleges may be formed and fashioned. The ancients had their view, the enlightened have their understanding, the pragmatic have their perspective, and the critical have their own interpretation. Furthermore, each chapter implicitly suggests a subsequent view of human personhood, what's wrong with people, what will "fix" them, and what the good life is all about. In other words, as Parker Palmer explains, "The way we diagnose our student's condition will determine the kind of remedy we offer."[1] What follows is a bit of a caricature and painting with broad brush strokes, but it will be a reflection of what has been covered thus far.

In the ancient tradition, students were viewed as souls who were formed regarding faith. The problem was sin, and the solution was God-inspired knowledge. Faith commitments drove the educational task. Theology was called the "Queen of the Sciences" which interpreted all of a student's previous knowledge. After all the "secular" subjects were studied, theology could piece them together in a united whole. There is much to commend in approaching education in a Bible-centric way, but the founders of American universities quickly abandoned this approach to the growing tide of secularism. Often, early education was sectarian, rigid, and restrictive.

This growing secularism and the influence of René Descartes and Immanuel Kant gave birth to what I've called "The College for Thinkers" or the "City of Big Brains." In this construct, human beings were viewed as "thinking things" or as materialist minds. Parker Palmer suggests that the problem with this approach is that students are considered "brain dead" and that the dominant treatment is to "drip data bits into our students' veins, wheeling comatose from one information source to the next . . . until they have graduated—and paid their tuition in full."[2] This view of personhood emphasizes the cognitive content and the scientific method. Moral formation is equated to scientific formation. The good life is the scientific life. As Plato suggests, "The unexamined life is not worth living."[3] However, this philosophy has bled into a hyper-examined life where everything is doubted. In biblical terms, one is "always learning but never able to arrive at a knowledge of the truth" (2 Tim. 3:7). There is much to appreciate in this period, but as noted, this type of college morphed from offering a right value of reason to what David Brooks calls an "elephantiasis of reason."[4] Christian education has shown itself to be susceptible to the College for Thinkers. In his influential book, Harry Blamires takes an Enlightenment outlook when he suggests, "The Christian mind is the prerequisite to Christian thinking. And Christian thinking is the prerequisite to Christian action."[5] Blamires adopts a reduced image of personhood and a flattened theory of knowledge—as if more knowledge produced Christian virtue. However, thinking the correct bits of information do not necessarily lead to a Christian way of being in the world.

The next City of temptation was the City of "Success", which idolized the economic man, or the utilitarian individual. In this view, personhood is reduced to employability. The problem is a non-thriving economy, and the solution is an education that produces better job skills. Life is about labor, and the truly successful life is the prosperous life. In this pragmatic view of education, there is no inherent value in learning. It is solely a means of getting a better job and being a more effective cog in the economy. Many of the attempts in educational systems that lean in this direction are oriented around job skills and market transferability. With this emphasis, colleges cater to employers who want college graduates with marketable skills, which are of a very specific, disciplinary type. There is little care for universal curriculum or collective knowledge—education is just to build a better resume. The pilgrimage in the City of "Success" never teaches you to care for the places that nurtured you but always takes you somewhere else—to the big city, better job, or higher pay.

Finally, in the City of Authenticity, schools have shifted to a view of personhood as expressive individuals. Here, feelings define humanity and remain supreme, and any attack on one's understanding of truth is an offense. Critique is a power play and is viewed as a form of attack. In this scheme, doubt is the posture of the student. The greatest fear and threat are hurt feelings, and the remedy is authenticity (be who you are). The good life is the comfortable life.

Each of the preceding chapters explored those who took a good narrative and made it ultimate; in a real sense, they made one aspect of the educational task a "god." While each development added something unique and needed in the educational task, taken to the extreme they are in error. Neither reason nor pragmatism nor authenticity can hold the full weight of an educational philosophy. I have argued, drawing on the contributions of St. Augustine, that humans are lovers and that the truly happy life, the flourishing life, is found in loving God and loving your neighbor. The problem for every person is disordered love, and that to be truly human is to experience and orientate one's love toward God. The solution to this quandary is ordered love. This thoroughly Augustinian view of humanity and purpose considers the former emphasis in each city as means to enjoy and love God. Reason serves what one loves. A vocation can serve the Kingdom of God. Feelings are important in one's affection toward God. A proper education holistically forms students in all these ways but does so by the redemptive love of Christ.

Perhaps the poet and scholar Wendell Berry says it best:

> The thing being made in a university is humanity...What universities...are *mandated* to make or to help to make is human beings in the fullest sense of those words—not just trained workers or knowledgeable citizens but responsible heirs of human culture...Underlying the idea of a university—the bringing together, the combining into one, of all the disciplines—is the idea that good work and good citizenship are the inevitable by-products of the making of a good—that is, a fully developed—human being.[6]

A proper Christian college experience ought to be approached in a humanistic way. That is, Christian education accounts for the reality of humanness and the underlying image of God in each subject. The reality of Christ is not the only truth there is, but it is the orienting truth through which the Christian interprets everything else. As love is ordered and expanded, we become more fully flourishing—more alive to the life we have been given.

Professor Joseph Clair argues that a holistic, liberal arts education answers four questions: who or what should I worship? (spiritual question—the Christian liberal arts); what should I know? (intellectual question—the College for Thinkers); what should I make? (vocational question—the College for Workers); and what should I be? (moral question—the College for Critics).[7] These questions are necessary but insufficient. The crucial question to ponder during your college years is, "What do I love?" In the tradition of Jesus and Augustine after Him, the answer for a good life is God and your neighbor. This response is not to neglect those other important questions but seeks to root those previous questions in a more holistic framework.

Now, with our bearings about us, we set on the educational pilgrimage with a better idea of our purpose and goals. We have a vision of our destination: ordering and expanding what and how we love. This provides a launching point and foundation for the rest of our lives after college, as well. If that's true, how does the destination re-orientate us on the journey? How should we travel the paths we take now in the college years? Part Two will provide some ways to reimagine and hopefully enliven your college voyage.

Keep traveling, pilgrim. We're not home yet.

Discussion Questions

1. Evaluate your college's vision or mission statement. What emphasis does your college place on education based on the six previous college types? Are there words that align with "thinkers" or "workers" or "critics" or "lovers"?

2. What is limited in each college types' vision of an educated person? What do you think they get right? What questions are answered? What questions remain unanswered?

Notes

1. Parker Palmer, *The Courage to Teach: Exploring the Inner Landscape of a Teacher's Life* (San Francisco: Jossey-Bass, 2007), 91.

2. Palmer, *The Courage to Teach*, 41-42.

3. Plato, *Plato's Apology of Socrates: An Interpretation with a New Translation*, trans. Thomas West (Ithaca, NY: Cornell University Press, 1979), 38a5-6.

4. David Brooks, *The Social Animal: The Hidden Sources of Love, Character, and Achievement* (New York: Random House, 2011), 226.

5. Harry Blamires, *The Christian Mind: How Should a Christian Think?* (Ann Arbor, MI: Servant, 1963), 3.

6. Wendell Berry, *Home Economics* (San Francisco: North Point Press, 1987), 77.

7. Joseph Clair, *On Education, Formation, Citizenship, and the Lost Purpose of Learning* (London: Bloomsbury, 2018), 1-33.

CHAPTER 7

Learning as Gift: Grace as The Foundation of Learning

"When I hear people say they have no religious impulse whatsoever...I always want to respond: Really? You have never felt overwhelmed by, and in some way inadequate to, an experience in your life, have never felt something in yourself staking a claim beyond yourself, some wordless mystery straining through words to reach you? *Never?*...Religion is what you do with these moments of overmastery in your life."

Christian Wiman, *My Bright Abyss*

"It is a triumph of science to have, in some degree, described the electron, and preposterous to suggest it has been explained."

Marilynne Robinson, *The Givenness of Things*

Where are you going? This is a question I've asked several times in different ways throughout this book. Your destination will affect how you travel the way. I've argued that love is the ultimate goal and motivation for learning. We order and expand our loves through cultivating our whole human person.

But the question of where we are going is also dictated by what story we tell ourselves. One of those quotations that haunts me—that keeps churning in my mind—is from Alasdair MacIntyre. He wrote, "I can only answer the question 'What am I to do?' if I can answer the prior question 'Of what story or stories do I find myself a part?'"[1] The question of action is tied to the question of story. How we pursue an education has everything to do with how we imagine the world.

When I was growing up, imagination seemed like a silly thing. Imagination implied words like: childish, fake, or immature. I wanted to be grown and being grown meant being *reasonable.* I wanted arguments, rationales, and deep thinking. Imagination seemed trivial and emotional. Stories and narratives were for kids.

However, story is exactly what we live by. The problem with those previous "cities" is that they told different stories, stories that were not true. To place a Christian in the story of intellectualism will not be sufficient to change the story. For example, I grew up imagining that the Christian story was heady. I lived in my brain. I could explain precise, doctrinal concepts to my peers. The evangelistic task was the apologetic task: defending the faith. I developed rational arguments for the existence of God. I could tell people how wrong they were and how right I was. But even if I knew all the right doctrinal beliefs, I had trouble living them out. Or more accurately, I did not really care to live them out, because I was right. And being right was enough. I had become a victim of the scientism of my day—the temptation in the College for Thinkers applied to my Christianity. I think you can see this reality in the YouTube or TikTok world. He "owned" his "opponent." She "destroyed" him with logic. Language matters. People are not persons; they're opponents. Arguments are not after truth; they are about embarrassing the other side. In an effort to be right, goodness and beauty fall by the wayside. Who cares if I'm kind as long as I'm right? Values flow from the story we tell.

Or if the story we narrate our lives by is one of success, then achievement is what we want. So, we can live as Christians and make decent decisions and be kind but what animates us is getting ahead. The story we tell ourselves is that we are behind, and the reason we work hard is to fulfill our dreams—upwardly mobile with nice cars in nice neighbors in nice schools. Christians can live this story, but it won't create much impact. We just live the cultural story we are told, and so we act much like culture. We must answer the question of what story we are a part of before we can answer the question of what we are to do.

The Importance and Limitations of Worldview

The popular term for how we tell the story of the world is worldview. I referenced this term in Chapter 2 about the distinct story of the Christian college. It's the glasses with which we "view" the "world." (See what they did there?) Our worldview narrates the world. A worldview, as one author defines it, is "a conceptual scheme by which we consciously or unconsciously place or fit everything we believe and by which we interpret and judge reality."[2] This conceptual scheme is a set of beliefs through which we live and evaluate the world. As popularly described, worldview is a set of glasses by which we see the world. Everyone has a worldview; the Christian college's task is to consciously form and construct a good, clear sets of glasses for you to view the world.

A worldview includes all the elements of a good story: a beginning, rising tension, climax, and resolution. A Christian worldview includes a beginning. We are created by God in his image. We are made to reflect God's image to the world around us. But here's the tension: we don't. Our ancient parents, Adam and Eve, fell from that state of perpetual grace and now we destroy rather than build, disintegrate rather than integrate, sin rather than be righteous. The Fall is embedded within us and within our cultural structures. The whole world groans inwardly because things are not the way they are supposed to be. The rest of history rises with the tension of sin. We are disordered seeking order. We are restless seeking rest. We hope for a Savior but people let us down. The climax, of course, is God sending his Son Jesus into the world to save us from sin. We are saved from ourselves by an outside influence. We are not good, yet God, in his mercy, saves us even while we were His enemies. Amazing! And the resolution is that God is now re-making all things and invites us into this story. Notice our part in the story. We are a small but important part. The story is about God rescuing his creation through Jesus Christ and the ongoing work of the Holy Spirit. We get to play a part and participate with God, but the world is not about us. We are decentralized in this story. Before you existed, the story was going on. After you die, the story will continue on. Whether you believe this story or not does not matter—it is the true story of the whole world for all times and for all people. This story is the worldview that animates a Christian college.

While it is necessary to be re-narrated from our cultural stories, worldview has some limits. (For starters, it is a bit presumptuous to assume we can arrive at this point of "the" biblical or Christian worldview). But our articulated beliefs and our actions that flow from those beliefs can be complicated. For example, a Christian may think, "No one can tell me what to do." She may have a clear, articulated theology. She may say, "Jesus is Lord." She may think, "Jesus must increase; I must decrease." But the idea of submitting to some authority seems unthinkable—whether that authority be in the home as a parent, in school as an administrator, or in church as a ministry leader. Not listening to anyone but ourselves seems as natural as breathing—it's how we imagine the world because we live in a story where we are central. Even if we have the intellectual belief that Jesus is Lord, the Western and American story that elevates the individual is the controlling narrative. It seems like these ideas are just the way things are, but they are picked up and absorbed in our world more than they are explained or taught. Our believed theology sometimes does not work its way down to our lived theology.

Likewise, when the popular imagination of education is constructing knowledge, then worldview is just one more field of study. Worldview has turned into a belief system we configure rather than its original meaning.[3] Worldview can seem like a cognitive exercise to add onto our education. Recently, a student asked why we have to study this spiritual subject on top of "regular" learning. Does the Christian college require more of their students than public school? The recent development of worldview thinking, then, assumes two different realms or types of knowledge: the human stuff and then the spiritual stuff. So, the idea goes, the Christian college is doing this spiritual addition that public or state schools do not do. However, this understanding presumes that the non-religious university does not have a worldview. But they do—even if they do not articulate it. Everyone assumes some conception of the world.

Acting well in the world means we need a story that tells us who we are and what to value. A worldview is necessary and unavoidable. But I want to add a deeper layer to worldview.

Knowledge as Gift

We live in a world full of gifts. I do not see a dandelion, for example, and then start extrapolating ideas from it. A dandelion comes as a gift before I start thinking about it or its various uses. Flowers do not have an entry fee to see. The flower existed and is there for me to view. The problem is that when I fail to notice it, I fail to appreciate it. And in an education directed toward love, to fail to appreciate is a failure to learn.

Our world is full of wonder and awe. God is the giver. That's the first premise of the Bible, and the first experience of life. We did not earn the right to exist. Our parents—even if they tried to nurture you—did not create you. You were given to them as a gift to receive. Your first breath was not paid or exchanged for but freely given. From your first heartbeat in the womb, the whole world has been God's gift.

And humanity is the recipient of the divine gift. We do not muster strength to gain the gift; we receive it. We don't earn it or philosophize about it, at least at first. This giftedness of the world can make sense of our "ah ha!" moments in the classroom. When something we did not know becomes something we do know, there is often a moment of delight at that discovery. But the thing did not change; we did. We began to see it. We became able to see more than we previously saw before, and it brings joy, wonder, and astonishment—and sometimes grief and dismay. This discovery as delight bears the likeness of a divine gift. We may describe our "ah ha!" moment but we can never exhaustively explain it. All things are understood in relation to the Giver and Creator, and we never fully understand anything unless we see this connection to Him.

So, the world is a theater of God's glory. God was not forced or coerced into revealing Himself. He chose to. One way that God chooses to reveal Himself is through created things. As such, all of creation is a gift. The letter to the Colossians has this great hymn where the apostle Paul writes of Christ, "For by Him all things were created, in heaven and on earth, visible and invisible, whether thrones or dominions or rulers or authorities—all things were created through Him and for Him. And He is before all things, and in Him all things hold together" (Col. 1:16-17). In other words, Christ is present wherever our eyes turn.

Perhaps we can rescue the language of worldview, or perhaps we need another term.

Restory-ing a Sacramental Vision

I want to advocate for a deeper, more basic orientation to the world than the modern conceptions of worldview can provide. The limitations of worldview need a fundamental shift in how we approach the world. My term is a sacramental imagination. In sacramental imagination, learning is not an effort to be won, but a gift to be received. The idea of sacramental imagination proposes that before we conceptualize or philosophize about something, we imagine it. Whereas worldview is compared to glasses that one puts on (to continue the ocular metaphor) a sacramental vision is like Lasik surgery that adjusts how we see the world before we put worldview glasses on. Because of the Fall and indwelling sin, we will always need to put the glasses on. But we also need a fundamental shift in how we see the world.

The way Christians sometimes use worldview focuses on *what* one believes. A sacramental vision emphasizes *how* one sees, a sort of intuition about the world. We approach the world with a certain disposition before we start articulating truths about the world. Before you can cognitively plot out your intellectual commitments, there is a way of relating to truth. What I'm suggesting is a way of education that is a way of imagining the world before we know it. Learning is less a construction to be created and more a gift to be found in unexpected places.

Let me take a moment to define "sacrament." The most popular definition of a sacrament comes from our old friend St. Augustine. He asserts that a sacrament is an outward and visible sign of an inward and invisible grace. In Protestantism, the sacraments include two things: baptism and the Lord's Supper. So, in baptism, we have water—an outward visible, thing—that signifies or points to the cleansing power of invisible grace. You are washed from your sins and made clean in Jesus Christ. The visible bread and wine represent the body and blood of Jesus who feeds the church with the grace of Himself. Though important in their materiality, one's eyes are not focused on water, bread, or wine as the main thing; we are supposed to see through them to the grace that lies behind and beyond them. This idea of seeing through ordinary, visible objects to the sacred reality behind them is key to a sacramental vision. It's my contention that when we cut out a sacramental imagination from the life of the church, we diminish our full understanding of the world. The world is full of wonder if we have eyes to see.

All things are infused with God's presence. A sacramental understanding of the world is to affirm that "God reveals himself through created things...that God can speak through the things He created."[4] In other words, all things shine with the light and splendor of God's grace. The sacraments give educators a new vision of the world. To beckon Marilynne Robinson's quote on the title page of this chapter, you can describe an electron, but it's foolish to say you've explained it. Robinson points out that scientists can describe the movements of electrons, how they function, their relation to protons and neutrons, etc. But electrons also invite wonder and mystery. Scientists can't exhaustively explain electrons.

In the mystic tradition, nature is God's book through which He can be contemplated indirectly. While God is most directly known through the Bible and the sacraments, God can also be known indirectly through the material and immaterial things He made. This stems from passages like Psalm 19, which begins, "The heavens declare the glory of God, and the sky above proclaims his handiwork." All of creation declares the glory of God. If that's true, then every human subject declares the glory of God. Romans 1 reads, "For what can be known about God is plain to them, because God has shown it to them. For his invisible attributes, namely, his eternal power and divine nature, have been clearly perceived, ever since the creation of the world, in the things that have been made. So they are without excuse" (v. 19-20). Even for the person who does not have the Scriptures, creation is singing out evidences of God. If we contemplate creation—slowing down to see its beauty, power, and divine nature—it can lead us to see the Creator. So, as one Eastern Orthodox writer puts it, "It is to see God in all things and all things in God—to discern, in and through each created reality, the divine presence that is within it and at the same time beyond it. It is to treat each thing as a sacrament, to view the whole of nature as God's book."[5] Everything you see and experience is God's gift and grace to you, so that you may know and see God both in and through ordinary, material and immaterial things.

Just as we see through the particular sacraments to the divine grace behind them, so all of created reality is revelatory—it reveals something about God. There is a shared holiness in created things as they share in their Creator. God creates with his imprint in a similar way that pottery bears the mark of the potter. Ordinary things are not to be enjoyed as ultimate but to be used en route to the ultimate enjoyment: God. God speaks through created things, which bestows worth, dignity, and a sense of holiness to those things—even ordinary things like a Tuesday math class or a dissected frog. St. Basil of Caesarea imagines the world as a school where we learn about God. He wrote that all creation is "the school where reasonable souls exercise themselves, the training ground where they learn to know God; since by the sight of visible and sensible things the mind is led, as by a hand, to the contemplation of invisible things."[6] A sacramental imagination invites such training.

An education understood as a gift needs to consider not only the content of learning or the curation of knowledge, but the imagination as well. The Reformed theologian and philosopher Calvin Seerveld advocates for the importance of the imagination in schooling. He defines good teaching as "teaching which captivates students and opens them up to God's world and his mighty acts in history…(one) fascinated by one's own material who is himself or herself a 'captivating' teacher, that is, one able to stir the imagination of students."[7] The first step of a good student is a personal one: do you find the wonder of your subject? If not, you haven't truly known it or learned it, at least not yet. In another place, Seerveld describes an aesthetic education—that is, an education that emphasizes the senses—as nurturing students

to the fact that God is still up to his marvelous tricks.
These students are cajoled into wonder at what meets their
senses, expectant about what they are experiencing. Teachers who cultivate this aesthetic imagination love their subject and love their students in a bond of trust. They love the
world to which God calls them.

Christ coming to us in human flesh in his incarnation
highlights the sacramental nature of the world: God has come
near to us in Christ, so one can expect God to be near in all
created things. The early Christian saint, St. John of Damascus wrote, "Because of [the incarnation], I salute all remaining
matter with reverence."[8] Here's but one example: last month,
my neighbor brought over caterpillars turning into chrysalides, which eventually turned into monarchs before migrating
to Mexico. She let us watch the different stages, and when I
say "us," I mean it was mainly for my children. But I watched
with child-like wonder. Did you know chrysalides have gold
flakes? I'm sure some scientists can describe why that is or
what function they serve, but they'll never *really* explain it
(to hearken back to Robinson's distinction). Sometimes, I
think God is more playful than I imagine Him. To me, this
was just one object lesson outside my discipline where my experience of something totally "secular" was infused with the
holy and sacred, where something seemingly ordinary turned
into a real presence. The chrysalis was not divine grace, but it
taught me to see through and beyond the thing to the divine.
The chrysalis did not change, but my ability changed to pay
attention and to see the divine glory in creation. It was there
all along free for me to notice.

Knowledge and *Gnosis*

Rather than mere knowledge of the material world or
bare facts, I want to suggest a different kind of knowing

called *gnosis*. To suggest *gnosis* as a type of knowledge is not to equate it with the early Christian heresy of Gnosticism. Gnosticism taught there were two knowledges exclusive to each other, thus leading to a dichotomy between body and spirit. The spirit was good, and the body was bad. Commenting on the church father Irenaeus, the monk Thomas Merton remarked, "All the faithful can and should be gnostics." *Gnosis* is not a term of special knowledge but a knowledge for all to pursue. In short, Merton continues, "Gnosis, the study of scripture and contemplation of its mysteries, shows Christ at the center of all history, and focuses on recapitulation, the summing up of all in the power of the divine mercy uniting to God in Him."[9] *Gnosis,* then, suggests a deeper knowledge to bring a wholeness to knowing rather than the separation that modern knowing and Gnosticism both encourage. It's not looking at the material fact alone or ignoring the material altogether. But like the sacraments, both the material and the spiritual matter. We look at and through the material to arrive at a holistic knowledge. *Gnosis* is a kind of knowledge, but a knowledge that leaves room for mystery—like prayer or contemplation. In this type of knowledge, you never master knowledge.

Relating *gnosis* to an academic subject, you can know something like math in a real way but also in a mysterious way or one that leaves you in awe. Let's take something easy as an example. Two plus two equals four. Pretty simple. You know it. But even in this simplistic example, two plus two equals four is not exhaustive. Why does two plus two equal four? What does it say about chaos and order? How can it lead to worship? In essence, *gnosis* knowledge leads to awe instead of pride. The same principle of *gnosis* can be applied to biology, literature, history, and communications. You will learn facts. You will know things. But knowledge takes you to *gnosis*: to deeper mystery beyond mere facts.

This contemplative learning invites a greater intimacy with your subject. Rather than maintain "academic distance" and "mastering" concepts, *gnosis* lovingly looks at a concept or subject—like a botanist in a lab studying a plant, or a Bible scholar returning to the text again and again, or a psychologist spending time with a patient and asking questions. By repetition and returning, the learner begins to see new things. Often, insight does not come from moving on to new subjects after a brief glance but from coming back to see the same thing in a different way. You will be rewarded for patience, time, and discipline rather than a mass of new information.

A Sacramental Vocation

The giftedness of creation also reorients us to how we see our vocation. As described earlier in the chapter on The City for Workers, an important part of college is preparing you for your vocation or calling. God has uniquely gifted, called, and equipped you to do your work in the world. However, much of life does not seem to be very life-changing. You may start out at an entry-level job that is far from your dream job. What do you make of vocation when your calling seems so trivial?

To describe a sacramental view of vocation, I want to employ Disney's *Soul* directed by Pete Doctor.[10] In *Soul*, Joe Gardner (voiced by Jamie Foxx) is a middle-aged black man who experiences a sort of mid-life crisis. He dreams of being a jazz pianist, but for now he's teaching band part-time to indifferent (and untalented) middle schoolers. He's offered the stability of going full-time, but he is hesitant. Is this an end to his dreams?

While he's considering the job and being urged by his mother to do the "responsible thing," Joe finally catches his big break: a gig with the famed Dorothea Williams (voiced by Angela Bassett). On the way back from his audition, he's skipping through the streets in exuberance, chatting away on the phone and...falls into a manhole. This misstep takes him on a journey to another world, to the place where souls separate from bodies and the dead are absorbed into the greater light. Joe slips out of his impending annihilation to a place where new souls are developed and nurtured before they enter existence. Here, he meets an emerging soul known as "22" (voiced by Tina Fey). She's been trained by the greatest minds to ever live, but she just doesn't think life is worth all the effort. She would rather drift back into non-existence.

As Joe is helping 22 find her desire to live, he has a chance to review his life, and he begins to realize that it has all been meaningless. He hasn't made a difference. He was made for music, but he hasn't pursued it or found fulfillment. He hasn't accomplished his vocation.

In the film, a constant refrain is finding one's special "spark." Everyone needs to identify the thing that makes their life worth living. Of course, the idea of a spark subjectifies the concept of vocation—rather than an external call, a spark is merely a subjective feeling. Music is Joe's spark. It's been his passion since he was 12 years old. It's what he lives for, what he gets lost in. As he realizes this, Joe is also out to help 22 discover her own spark, even though she would rather not. This pursuit takes them on a journey that I won't spoil for you.

One of the things that *Soul* demonstrates is Joe's (and our) overemphasis on vocation. In Christian communities as well as in the secular sphere, I fear we've oversold vocation as a sort of golden ticket to a meaningful life—as if we can just pick the right career that inspires our "spark" and we will be happy. But what if life is more than a job? What if there's more to fulfillment?

Joe comes to his senses in a strange way: he achieves everything he dreamed. He gets to experience the perfect gig with Dorothea Williams. Here's his big break. He gets everything he wanted. He's lifted toward transcendence. As he leaves the club, he asks, "What now?" Dorothea responds, "Come back tomorrow and we do it again." Joe walks away disappointed. That's it? That's what he's been longing for?

The bodiless 22 teaches Joe something in their travels together. It's this sacramental secret: being is a good in itself. Life is a gift—we can see through ordinary events to a sacredness that lies behind. What gives 22 her "spark," and what wakes Joe up, is seeing one of those helicopter leaves fall from a tree. This recollection ignites a trip down memory lane for Joe: eating pizza, helping others find their sparks, sand between his toes on the beach, fireworks, breathing fresh air on a bike ride. He remembers something 22 said to him, "Maybe sky watching can be my spark…or walking! I'm really good at walking!" To which he replied, "Those really aren't purposes, 22. That's just regular old living."

Just *living*. Perhaps because it's regular and old, we tend to forget about it. But isn't life itself something amazing? *Soul* encourages the viewer—imperfectly yet resolutely—to embrace a holy indifference to what we are doing in a given moment or season and a divine passion for simply being. What we do is important—profoundly so. But perhaps what we do is less important than how we see.

To say I love what I get to do during the day is an understatement. I can't imagine truly flourishing doing anything else. For me, educating college students aligns with all the ways of defining a vocation. I have a passion for it.

There's a need. There's communal affirmation. I feel called to it. But more than likely, there will be a time when my vocation, the thing that gives me meaning and purpose and "spark," will be ripped away because of budget cuts or closure or a pandemic. In that moment, I could wander like a lost soul (another feature of the film) and wonder, "What kind of life is this?"

Or I can look at the world and see my exhausting but joyful kids, or my lovely wife, or the mountain views from our backyard, or the taste of pizza, and think: "What kind of life is *this*?" The first is a question of despair; the second is a question of grace. How I answer will depend on what I want to see, and on what kind of training my eyes have received.

Seeing life as a sacramental gift beckons us to ask the second question—the question of grace.

Conclusion

A sacramental vision requires a shift in our fundamental approach to the world rather than simply articulating a Christian worldview. It encourages a reimagining of what life is, and therefore, what the classroom space and learning environment is. In essence, as one sees through the ordinary means of bread, wine, and water to divine reality and grace to which they point, so teachers and students can see through subjects, disciplines, and lessons to the divine creator behind them.

The theologian Hans Urs von Balthasar diagnoses the modern culture as characterized by "a fateful loss of sight" in which "the light of Being no longer shines over the world."[11] In many ways, modern knowing attempts to purge God's presence from creation and our view of reality (as if such a thing were possible). However, education is an occasion to see God as the light which enlightens everything—not just certain subjects, certain arenas, or certain things. The whole world is an epiphany of God. The particular sacraments are the unveiling of God's glory hidden in water, bread, and wine, and when eyes turn toward other ordinary objects—a subject, a fellow student, or a classroom—one has the vision to behold divine gifts for what they really are.

We can describe our discoveries as gifts, but we can never explain them. There is an inherent mystery and "more-ness." By having this sacramental imagination, you as a student can train your eyes to see the world shining like a gift to be discovered. God is still at work playing tricks. Studying history, science, literature, engineering, or theology should lead you to understand that there is something more there, behind and beyond the subject. God doesn't just fit in the gap but infuses the whole enterprise. There is something like a mystery of existence—the sublime goodness and absurdity of it all. The restoration of sight requires a reimagining of the world in which we live.

What if we imagined our learning not as knowledge to be manipulated and mastered but as a gift to be received and loved? In a central passage in *The Spirit of Medieval Philosophy*, Étienne Gilson contends that for Christians, the universe is most simply "a sum total of creatures owing their existence to an act of love"—the act of a creator who, "being charity... lives by charity." Gilson imagines love flowing through the universe "like the life-giving blood through the body."[12] What if we, as Christians, were those marked by the life-giving feature of the universe? The love-oriented Savior dwelt personally among us by grace so that we may know Him and His world. The pattern of the gift-giving Christ ought to influence our learning.

Discussion Questions

1. Describe a time (if any!) when education or a discovery brought you delight.
2. Think about your own academic discipline. How does faith relate to your subject? How might Christianity affect your field of study and vocation?
3. Define a sacramental imagination in contrast to a worldview.
4. What do you think Marilynne Robinson means when she says, "It is a triumph of science to have, in some degree, described the electron, and preposterous to suggest is has been explained"?
5. Describe a few ways or a few moments where you felt "overwhelmed by grace" or found the goodness of existence in unexpected ways.

Notes

1. Alasdair MacIntyre, *After Virtue: A Study in Moral Theory* (Notre Dame, IN: Notre Dame University Press, 1984), 216.

2. Ronald Nash, *Worldview in Conflict: Choosing Christianity in a World of Ideas* (Grand Rapids: Zondervan, 1992), 16.

3. Worldview is a conflicted and contested term. Originally, it was something like a default setting for a culture or people. "Lifeview" was a more personal story or particular lens. But for both, this view of the world was most often pre-theoretical and before articulation. Perhaps there are so many definitions or ideas that the term has become rather vacuous.

4. Leonard Vander Zee, *Christ Baptism and the Lord's Supper: Recovering the Sacraments for Evangelical Worship* (Downers Grove, IL: InterVarsity Press, 2004), 17.

5. Kallistos Ware, "Ways of Prayer and Contemplation," in *Christian Spirituality: Origins to the Twelfth Century*, Bernard McGinn and John Meyendorff, eds. (New York: Crossroad, 1985), 398.

6. Basil of Caesarea, *Hexameron* in *Nicene and Post-Nicene Fathers*, 2nd series, Bloomfield Jackson, ed. And trans. (Grand Rapids: Eerdmans, 1983), 8:52.

7. Calvin Seerveld, *Rainbows for a Fallen World: Aesthetic Life and Artistic Task* (Toronto: Toronto Tuppence Press, 2005), 139.

8. St. John of Damascus, *First Apology Against Those Who Attack the Divine Images*. Trans. David Anderson. (Crestwood, NY: St. Vladimir's Seminary Press, 1980), 1.4.

9. Thomas Merton, *A Course on Christian Mysticism* (Collegeville, MN: Liturgical Press, 2017), 29.

10. What follows is derived from an article I wrote for an online newsletter at Fare Forward. See Alex Sosler, "Soul," *Fare Forward*, January 6, 2021: https://farefwd.com/index.php/2021/01/06/soul/.

11. Hans Urs von Balthasar, *The Glory of the Lord: A Theological Aesthetics*, vol 1., *Seeing the Form* (San Francisco: Ignatius Press, 2009), 624.

12. Quoted by Eric Miller in "Reign of Love" *Commonweal Magazine*. Published January 2, 2019, https://www.commonwealmagazine.org/reign-love.

CHAPTER 8

Learning by Charity:
Love as the Posture of Learning

"Knowledge is valuable only when charity informs it."

Augustine, *City of God*

The great musician Tina Turner once wrote a song that asked a question: "What's love got to do with it?" This may be the question you're asking. You've thought about loving your parents, loving your friends, loving tacos, and possibly loving a spouse one day. But loving learning or love as a means to learning? What's love got to do with *education*?

Love is a funny word. It doesn't sound funny (like bamboozle or hullaballoo). Its humor comes in its various and empty definitions. There's a sign that you may have seen in a neighborhood yard near you. "In this house, we believe:" the sign begins. "Science is real. Black lives matter. No human is illegal. Women's rights are human rights." I know these slogans are loaded with dogma, but in many

ways, Christians should and ought to affirm these truths.
Amen, neighbor!

But the sign also includes another mantra: "Love is love."
Again, I know there's a doctrine behind that statement, but it
makes you wonder: What is love anyway? Is it that self-evi-
dent that it's self-referential? It just is what it is? What help
is that? The meaning of love can be so murky that it's hard to
know where to start.

Love is…

If you've been to a wedding, you've likely heard 1 Corinthians 13 read. It's a classic wedding text because the chapter is on love. "Love is patient. Love is kind. It does not
envy or boast…" But 1 Corinthians 13 is not about marital
love, at least not at first. In context, the chapter on love is
about spiritual gifts. The apostle Paul is defining spiritual
gifts—prophecy, teaching, service, etc. But he says that the
great spiritual gift, the thing to be sought above all else, is
love. So, with spiritual gifts and knowledge in mind, let's
think about love.

The Greek word translated "love" replaced a more
ancient word. Historically, the Greek word had been translated "charity." So that "charity" is patient, kind, etc. Today,
charity may be a more confusing word than love. You may
think that charity means handouts to the poor—like giving
a dollar to a homeless person or going to serve in the soup
kitchen. It's something you could do, but otherwise it's more
of an add-on than a necessity. But the word charity has more
ancient roots. Charity as classically defined was rooted in a
moral obligation to love one's neighbor. When I consider
"charity" I am referring to the more historic sense of charity: a moral obligation to love whoever is in front of you.

Charity is a demand, and I want to suggest that charity is how one pursues the life of learning. As mentioned previously, that's what makes education a moral act and not just an intellectual task.

This spiritual gift of charity means that if you are a Christian, you have a responsibility and obligation to exert charity on whoever is in front of you. In the context of a college classroom that sometimes means the (boring) teacher lecturing in front of you, the (annoying) student beside you who does not understand the new concept, the (unexciting) author of the book you are reading, etc. You have a personal, moral obligation to live by charity in all of life—and that includes on the college campus.

So if the goal of life is one of ordered love, then education is not exempt from it. When a young lawyer asked, "Which is the greatest commandment?" and Jesus says, "You shall love the Lord your God with all your heart and with all your soul and with all your mind. This is the greatest and first commandment. And a second is like it: You shall love your neighbor as yourself. On these two commandments depend all the Law and the Prophets." Jesus does not put an asterisk after summarizing the goal of life and say "*except education." All of our lives are lived before God, so education contributes to a life of love.

The Means of Charity

If the Christian life, and therefore education, should be marked by charity, then it is not sufficient to be right or hold the truth. I would argue that it is not enough even to be good, but our goodness must affect how we hold and seek the truth. As Pope Paul VI describes in a document called "His Church,"

> It would indeed be a disgrace if our dialogue were
> marked by arrogance, the use of bared words or offensive
> bitterness. What gives it its authority is the fact that it
> affirms the truth, shares with others the gifts of charity, is
> itself an example of virtue, avoids peremptory language,
> makes no demands. It is peaceful, has no use for extreme
> methods, is patient under contradiction and inclines
> towards generosity.[1]

So often, I see Christians use the same "worldly" tactics as their neighbors rather than offering a distinct voice of mercy and love. YouTube advertises that someone "owned" them with #facts or "destroys" their opponent. I don't know about you, but I've never changed my mind because someone called me an idiot. Rather, like Jesus, I was patiently heard, loved, and understood even when I was wrong. And if we call ourselves Christians—literally "little Christs"—then perhaps we should take Jesus' posture in learning.

Everyone has a certain way of or rule for reading, interpreting, and listening. These ways or rules are called "hermeneutics." A hermeneutic includes certain guiding postures and questions that you have as you approach and interpret a text or person. How should you be listening? What should you be listening for? Those are hermeneutical questions. Using a hermeneutic of suspicion tends to be the dominant paradigm of American higher education in the twenty-first century as mentioned in the College for Critics chapter. In essence, the way to learn in the modern consciousness is to read by a set of rules that question, critique, and search for lies. The scholar's imagination is to "critically think" and take apart. There is a correct stage of asking critical questions, but I want to suggest that it is a poor disposition to learn. In other words, critique is a part of good thinking, but if it is all you do—if it becomes your posture—then learning becomes dysfunctional. If you read or listen only with ears to refute, then there is no real listening taking place, because your mind is already made up. To be a charitable learner you must learn how to listen—and to listen well is to think. Charity is a better posture for learning because "love, not indifference, invites the real...Love presumes that the real is lovely or loveable or worth loving...What this is arguing is that love is what enables us to see things as they are and as they are meant to be."[2] Charity desires to put things together—even if it must take a few things apart. An education pursued in love wants to leave things better rather than in shambles.

The educator and mystic Parker Palmer, quoting two influential sources, takes it a step further: "In the words of Abraham Joshua Heschel . . .'It is impossible to find Truth without being in love.' In the words of St. Gregory, 'Love itself is knowledge; the more one loves the more one knows.'"[3] Not only is a hermeneutic of charity better than any prevailing model of learning, but with Palmer, I want to say that charity is the only means of truly knowing anything at all.

Here is where 1 Corinthians 13 comes in. As already discussed, the chapter of charity is about spiritual gifts, but it is also wrapped in knowledge language. To close, the chapter ends like this:

> For we know in part and we prophesy in part, but when the perfect comes, the partial will pass away. When I was a child, I spoke like a child, I thought like a child, I reasoned like a child. When I became a man, I gave up childish ways. For now we see in a mirror dimly, but then face to face. Now I know in part; then I shall know fully, even as I have been fully known. So now faith, hope, and love abide, these three; but the greatest of these is love. (1 Cor. 13:9-13)

For Paul, the spiritual gift of love connects to knowledge. Now we know in part, which brings a fundamental sense of humility. We will not know perfectly or completely. We see from a perspective that is culturally situated, family-formed, and communally shaped. We do not have omniscient knowledge like God—which means we can learn things from lots of different people and perspectives.

Just to remind you: love is not some good-vibe, get-along-with-each-other emotion. You will interact with people (if you haven't already!) who make you mad and who sometimes say hurtful or demeaning things. You and I need guidelines to help us in those moments when things get heated and passions get involved. Passion or care is not the problem, but how we interact reveals something deeper within us. So, as John Stott explains, "Love needs law to guide it. It is rather naïve to claim that love has no need of any direction outside itself...Love is not infallible. Indeed, it is sometimes blind. So, God has given us commandments to chart the pathways of love."[4] The definition of hermeneutics is a set of rules in approaching a text or topic. Rules serve as guidelines that direct the soul. They function as a type of guardrail or pathway for love. We need to be told, "This is what love looks like" or we will end up confused and say, "Love is love." Rather than a list of moral commands, Christians are called to the law of love (Gal. 5:1-6, 13-18; Rom. 13:10). As we read and listen, we ought to pursue ways of learning that are joyful, peaceful, patient, and kind. Kindness is a virtuous rule as you approach a text. Self-control should be displayed in responding to a book or fellow student.

Let me offer a modest definition of a hermeneutic of charity: a hermeneutic of charity is a humble, relational, and attentive posture toward a person, text, or topic that seeks to understand and so exhibit love to the person, text, or topic in order to build up the proper goal of life, which is to love God. This definition includes postures and acts (being humble, relational, attentional), subjects (persons, texts, topics) and goals (understanding, love). Here's what it means to live a life of love and what should mark your learning:

> If I speak in the tongues of men and of angels, but have not love, I am a noisy gong or a clanging cymbal. And if I have prophetic powers, and understand all mysteries and all knowledge, and if I have all faith, so as to remove mountains, but have not love, I am nothing. If I give away all I have, and if I deliver up my body to be burned, but have not love, I gain nothing.
>
> Love is patient and kind; love does not envy or boast; it is not arrogant or rude. It does not insist on its own way; it is not irritable or resentful; it does not rejoice at wrongdoing, but rejoices with the truth.
>
> Love bears all things, believes all things, hopes all things, endures all things.
>
> Love never ends. As for prophecies, they will pass away; as for tongues, they will cease; as for knowledge, it will pass away. (1 Cor. 13:1-8)

In essence, the apostle Paul is contending that you can pursue all the spiritual gifts (prophecy, speaking in tongues, service, teaching), but if you don't have the primary spiritual gift (love), then you don't have any spiritual gift—or at least any gift that will be edifying.

St. Paul says if you speak in tongues of angels but have not love, you are as annoying as a banging cymbal. Love is the only enduring, worthwhile gift to pursue. You may be the smartest person in the class, but if you have not love, you are as frustrating as a first-grader with a saxophone. You may have straight A's, but if you have not love, then you are nothing. You could be persecuted because you stood up for Jesus to someone, but if you have not love, you gain nothing. You can have the best degree that leads to the best job, but if you have not love, it's pointless. As I hope is clear, God, who is love, takes love seriously. It is the gift he wants to give you, and love is the gift we give to the world.

Not only is love for living, but as I'm suggesting, these are also educational virtues for learning. Charity informs how one knows; it is a posture the Christian takes in learning. It is not so much external rules we must follow, but a vision of a type of person we want to become. Charity infuses the learning task and affects the whole process.

Let me try to get as practical as I can by taking a few of the lines and applying it to the educational enterprise.

First, love is patient. The German theologian Hans Urs von Balthasar (that's a fun name) claimed that "patience is the first virtue of the one who wants to perceive. And the second is renunciation."[5] What he means is that if you want to understand, to truly see something, you need patience. The second thing you need is renunciation—to deny yourself or your initial impression. To understand an argument, to spend time listening to an opposing view one finds plain wrong or even disturbing, or to read a complicated book requires patience. You need to renounce yourself and what you think will delight you to spend time with an author or argument that you find complex or complicating. After having patience and renouncing your own desires, you may find that your desire has been changed or molded. When you try as hard as you can but cannot seem to comprehend a concept, you need to learn patience. When a classmate wants to rush to judgments and conclusions without hearing opposing views, he needs patience. Especially in a modern, tweetable, instant gratification culture, now more than ever, we need to be trained to be patient. And patience requires humility.

Secondly, love is discerning. Charity "does not rejoice at wrongdoing but rejoices with the truth." In the educational virtues, love does "not rejoice at wrong-knowing." In popular usage, love is constantly affirming, and it is impossible to love someone or something and disagree with them. Here's where Paul comes to redefine our notions of love. Love is not the same as having good feelings. That's not what love looks like in practice. Lots of people love you and disagree with you. Heck, I disagree with myself sometimes. Disagreement or conflict is not the problem. How we engage in and interact with conflict is what matters. What I don't mean to suggest is some sort of proposal like, "Can't we all just get along?" or "Let's be nice to one another!" or "You know, Pol Pot was probably a nice guy at heart, just misunderstood." Our modern view of love may conjure these sentiments but distorts the true meaning of love.

Cornelius Plantinga argues, "Discernment is a feature of wisdom, which is the main goal of higher education."[6] Paul prays for the Philippians that "your love may abound more and more, with knowledge and all discernment" (Phil. 1:9). He also instructs the Roman church: "Let love be genuine. Abhor what is evil; hold fast to what is good" (Rom. 12:9). Critical thinking is a great evaluative skill but a poor skill in seeking to understand. Knowing requires a critical element but always a loving stance. Discernment is a positive gesture where we seek the true, which includes a rejection of the false. Truth, at its essence, however, is not a sword to wield but a beauty to behold.

Lastly, the apostle Paul closes his list on love by concluding with faith, hope, and love. In essence, this sums up the educational task. Augustine is helpful in connecting these concepts:

> If faith falters, love itself decays. For if someone lapses in his faith, he inevitably lapses in his love as well, since he cannot love what he does not believe to be true. If on the other hand he both believes and loves, then by good conduct and by following the rules of good behavior he gives himself reason to hope that he will attain what he loves...But faith will be replaced by the sight of visible reality, and hope by the real happiness which we shall attain, whereas love will actually increase when these things pass away.[7]

Faith is the nature of the task of education: knowing truth, which includes the reasonable components of knowledge. As Augustine suggests, a knower must know something and believe it in order to love it. Hope can be seen as the means of love that draws humanity to character habits and rightly ordered loves. We have hope that we can know something. Finally, love is a classroom's happiness. It is always more passionately desired when obtained, and the task of the college years is to attain more of the love of God. Love is the eternal thing to be increasingly enjoyed.

Curiosity vs. Studiousness

St. Augustine makes a further distinction in the intellectual appetite. We all have a desire to know the truth. We want to follow the truth wherever it leads. We have an appetite for it. He labels two ways to pursue knowledge: curiosity and studiousness. He's a bit counterintuitive, so allow me to explain. Usually, we think curiosity is good, and studiousness is this bookish, nerdy posture. But not for Augustine. Augustine uses curiosity negatively as in "curiosity killed the cat." The curious person wants to discover everything and rid the world of unknowns, and this posture gets them into trouble. It seeks to control, dominate, and own new knowledge. Curious people hate what they do not know. This type of person seeks knowledge for the sake of pride and ambition.

As opposed to the curious person, St. Augustine recommends the studious person. This student seeks knowledge in love. They want to participate lovingly in the truth, not to own it, but to spread it. They relate to truth not as masters but as stewards. Knowledge is a gift to the studious as described in the last chapter. God gives a world full of gifts, and we discover them. Once we discover them, we want others to see the glories of creation and the grandeur of God. Learning is not so much earned in effort but is more like a revelation to be seen. Studious people seek to connect truth with other truths, to expand it, and to see the interconnectedness of the world.

While both attitudes and postures share the search for truth, they have different goals. The curious seeks knowledge out of anxiety and fear; the studious seeks knowledge from a place of love. The intellectual posture to develop is one of studiousness, by the means and goal of charity.

Conclusion

To seek understanding is the goal of love. In the quest for "objective truth," the modern agenda distances the learner from the subject and therefore distances understanding—like Bitzer rather than Sissy in Charles Dickens' *Hard Times*. But if love is the foundation of knowledge, then it starts with compassion and empathy for a person—whether he is the author, she is a classmate, or they are a research group. Love seeks true reality but is discerning enough to confess when a judgment is wrong. Mark Schwehn puts it like this: "Humility...does not mean uncritical acceptance: it means, in practical terms, the *presumption* of wisdom and authority *in the author*."[8] Charitable thinking is a humble pursuit of truth—not being afraid of what one will find nor afraid to call out error. The student can seek after truth and find it in the oddest of places. That's one reason why a liberal arts college does not limit their curriculum to only Christian authors. Christians have the best basis to pursue truth, but Christians do not have a monopoly on truth. God is gracious to reveal truth to anyone who seeks it, so sometimes secular or other non-Christian sources can help us see truth (and even God) more clearly.

After all, we serve a God that descended to us in the person of Jesus to be known. He did not have to. He chose to be known. And He opens truth to us as a gift to be uncovered. If Christ did that for us, then there ought to be a level of humility in us if we are called "Christians." Displaying charity means we do not overrate our powers of judgment or assume we know everything. Being charitable means we don't judge people by the worst they have ever said or done. Pursuing the path of charity means that we are always open to changing our minds, because we may be wrong, and we never close the door on the possibility of renewal or repentance.

Discussion Questions

1. In your own words, what is love? How would you describe the way love relates to education?

2. In small groups, read through 1 Corinthians 13. Outline some ways that this "chapter of love" could be applied to education in your college years. Come back together as a larger group to share.

3. There's an old addage, "Curiosity killed the cat." What do you think that means in regard to education? Do you think any knowledge is "off limits" or that there is anything that's not worth knowing? Why or why not?

Notes

1. Pope Paul VI, "Ecclesiam Suam", *Vatican,* August 6, 1964.

2. Esther Lightcap Meek, *Loving to Know: Introducing Covenant Epistemology* (Eugene, OR: Cascade, 2011), 435.

3. Parker Palmer, *To Know as We Are Known: Education as Spiritual Journey* (San Francisco: HarperOne, 1993), 57.

4. John Stott, *Christ the Controversialist: A Study in Some Essentials of Evangelical Religion* (Downers Grove, IL: InterVarsity Press, 1991), 161.

5. Hans Urs von Baltasar, *The Heart of the World* (San Francisco: Ignatius Press, 1980), 24.

6. Cornelius Plantinga, *Engaging God's World: A Christian Vision of Faith, Learning, and Living* (Grand Rapids: Eerdmans Press, 2002), 100.

7. Augustine, *On Christian Teaching,* trans. R. P. H. (New York: Oxford University Press, 1999), 28.

8. Mark Schwehn, *Exiles from Eden* (New York: Oxford University Press, 2005), 48, emphasis original.

CHAPTER 9

Learning as Belonging: Love as the Motive of Education

"God comes, aiming for ecstasy in the body of the creature. This must never be denied. To deny this is to undermine the central purpose of theological education—to give witness to God's embrace of the creature and the desire of God to make embrace the vocation of creatures that have yielded to the Spirit."

Willie James Jennings, *After Whiteness*

"There is in every person that which waits, waits, waits and listens for the sound of the genuine in herself. There is that in every person that waits—waits and listens—for the sound of the genuine in other people. And when these two sounds come together, this is the music God heard when He said, 'Let us make man in our image.'"

Howard Thurman, "The Sound of the Genuine"

There is something erotic about Christianity. Now, before you start calling me a pervert, let me explain myself. I'm not speaking of erotic films or deviant sexuality. Those are perversions of *eros*. Christianity comes with an urgent desire, a longing of the soul, an embodied ache in reaching to Jesus and to one another. Jesus is not indifferent and apathetic but passionate and affectionate.

The Christian story includes a virgin impregnated, Jesus weeping, a prostitute coming to wipe Jesus' feet with her tears, and the beloved disciple lying on the Savior's bosom. Jesus says, "This is my body. Take and eat." Tears. Desire. Body. Belonging. Scandal.

This erotic desire drives life together with God. If you're like me, then that word—"erotic"—makes you uncomfortable. It's too bodily, too sensual, and too emotional. The term has become commercialized and sexualized as if *eros* is latent with promiscuity and sin. But by erotic, I mean a strong, passionate, physical desire—something like soul aching or longing—like being in love for the first time. *Eros* simply means desire—and desire can be sexual and bodily, but it also exceeds the sensual. At the center of every human heart is an erotic desire: to be known and to know others. That's not a bad desire; it is a good, God-given desire. You have an appetite for knowledge, which is to say, you want something you do not have. See how often a question arises to be met with an immediate Google search. Your desire leads to seeking fulfillment: to be intimate with what you do not yet know.

Yale Divinity professor Willie James Jennings suggests an erotic education as an alternative to the college in which you find yourself. There's something in this modern academic project that rejects the erotic in favor of objectivity. Detach from relationships. Don't feel. Disconnect. Desire leads to delusion.

An emotional invitation to connect feels strange to me. As a white, male scholar in the Western World, I'd like to rid myself of any desire at all. I don't want to show or communicate "how I'm feeling." If I'm honest, though, this natural tendency in me to disconnect is dehumanizing—to myself and others. The posture causes me to dehumanize others and their feelings or their desires to belong. "Just toughen up. Be stronger. Be a better individual." It seeps through my education and profession and into my relationships—with those as intimate as my spouse and children. It trickles down to my Christianity as it morphs into some sort of Stoic-Buddhist ethic: "Conceal, don't feel" as Princess Elsa puts it in *Frozen*.

The dangers of emotionalism are strong and real. (Or in princess phrasing again, Anna has her own set of issues). Emotions are frequently manipulated and untrustworthy. But in the western academic environment, few people would caution the dangers of intellectualism. The way to think and the way to live are *eros*-less.

But longing leads to love as an expression of care, while lack of desire leads to abuse and exploitation. If we don't care about people, fellow students, or our neighbor—if there is no desire—then who cares how we treat them? As Christians, we ought to care about relationships, belonging, and togetherness.

Is there an eroticism fit for Christianity?

How you pursue knowing and being known by others can be messed up, though. St. Augustine says my love is my weight, or my love is my gravitational force.[1] It's not a question of if desire is right or wrong: to desire is human. It's also not a question of if desire will take us somewhere—it will. It is a matter of what rules our hearts and where our desires are pointed. If it's toward only earthy and temporal things, then our hearts will weigh us down and sink like a boulder in water. But if our desire, our *eros*, is on divine things, right realities, and true truths, then our hearts can long heavenward like flames from a fire. Rather than make us less human, right desire will make us more human and more aligned with all that God created us to be.

Moreover, proper desire can lead to commitment and something life-giving. Love gives birth to new life. At some point, you have looked at someone and thought, "I would like to get to know them"—there was an initial attraction that led to desire for more. This initial attraction—this erotic desire—is disordered if it is mere lust. If you only want to know someone else to manipulate them as a sexual plaything, then the erotic desire is disordered. But rightly ordered, this initial erotic desire leads to a lasting love—a marital, committed love. One of the natural outcomes of marriage is often new life—a baby. In a similar way, erotic desire for truth can give birth to understanding more truth and arriving at new discoveries. Desire is not an end but a starting point for a life-giving relationship. The question is which way your desire is pushing you. There is such a thing as good desire.

Knowledge as Personal and Relational

The perversion of the erotic is lust. Lust objectifies a person. As previously described, a person with lustful intentions does not view a person as an image bearer or a brother or sister; this other is reduced to a tool to manipulate for their own pleasure. To illustrate this concept with a term from last chapter, that's what the curious imagination does. It views knowledge as a thing to be owned, mastered, or conquered. The studious imagination is different. Studious students take that initial erotic desire as a gateway to love. The appetite to know is the same between the curious and the studious student but what they do with the knowledge is different. The studious student sees their role as a steward as they seek to care for what they know rather than use it and discard it. Erotic desire is perverted when you see a person as an "it" rather than a "you." Lust wants "it," while proper *eros* desires a beloved person.[2] The studious imagination sees a subject of knowledge as a "you" —as personal. Intimacy with truth leads to new life.

Let me try to translate this to the educational journey. There is a way to approach learning that is objective, detached, and dehumanizing—where we treat everything and person as an "it" rather than a personal "you." When we view things in view of caring for them, it has the possibility to be life-changing. On this idea, philosopher Esther Lightcap Meek summarizes a thought which originated with Jewish philosopher Martin Buber: "...but in the I-You relation, I and You are present to one another in a way that puts all else in the background. Rather than 'experiencing' the You, I behold it, encounter it, confront it, commune with it. In that encounter, I and You are present to one another in an enduring present."[3] True knowing, then, is an encounter. Truth is found in multiple encounters that form trust. This "I-You" encounter has the potential to change the knower. We rarely take long enough to investigate something that's an "it." In such a world, "it" is background noise, not worthy of our attention or notice. Maybe "it" is something that can lead us to look smarter or better, but an "it" is otherwise unimportant. Those who see reality as personal see the world as a gift, while those who see the world as an "it" see the world as an object. To arrive at knowledge is to arrive at a certain kind of intimacy between a subject and yourself.

Furthermore, knowing is rooted in truth and relationship. Parker Palmer explains truth's etymology: "The English word 'truth' comes from a Germanic root that also gives rise to our word "troth," as in the ancient marriage vow 'I pledge thee my troth.' With this word one person enters a covenant with another, a pledge to engage in a mutually accountable and transforming relationship, a relationship forged of trust and faith in the face of unknowable risks."[4] In other words, to know anything is a relational engagement. It requires passionate desire that leads to care in a communal trust.

Now, you may think that science does not work this way. The hard sciences are objective, not rooted in things like trust and relationship. Maybe this trust-talk applies to social subjects like history or psychology, but certainly not mathematics or chemistry or computer science. Math is just facts, my dude. However, here's what a renowned scientist, Michael Polanyi, argues: "Science will appear then as a vast system of beliefs, deeply rooted in our history and cultivated today by a specially organized part of our society (i.e., scientists). We shall see that science is not established by the acceptance of a formula, but is part of our mental life, shared out for cultivation among many thousands of specialized scientists throughout the world, and shared receptively, at second hand, by many millions."[5] In other words, even in science, what is true is what is trusted. Scientific organizations are made to certify trust. It is not a matter of whether we trust, but of who we trust and why.

With trust, Palmer again advocates that love is the foundation of knowledge:

> Knowledge originates in compassion, or love...The goal of a knowledge arising from love is the reunification and reconstruction of broken selves and worlds...The mind motivated by compassion reaches out to know as the heart reaches out to love. Here, the act of knowing is an act of love, the act of entering and embracing the

reality of the other, or allowing the other to enter and embrace our own.[6]

In a loving relationship with truth, the whole task of education and learning is wrapped in care or belonging. Care, or desire, should carry the knower and seeker. As Esther Lightcap Meek suggests, "To care is to move toward the unknown."[7] This is a beautiful picture of education. One should desire to know more, because they care—about the subject, about the author, about the teacher, about one's future relationships. Desire is the motive that carries the knower to the unknown. Love leads you outside of yourself to understand the world of another subject or person.

However, this does not mean that truth is wholly subjective. One of the disturbing developments on the modern university campus that we saw in the City of Authenticity is viewing every truth claim as a personal attack. If everything is relative, then there is no single truth. There are as many truths as there are diverse selves. While the individual is the discoverer of truth, the individual is not the arbitrator of truth. You do not get to decide what is true or not. I can say, "Well, I think rain is actually milk," but no matter how earnestly I believe that to be true, it does not accord with reality. But in such a climate where the prevailing ethos is subjective, relative truth, every argument becomes a personal attack. By arguing that "no, rain is not actually milk," you are trying to dominate me and make me submit to your reality.

I think you see the silliness in such an argument. Though truth is personal, we also need to affirm that truth is objective even if knowing is personal and subjective—it does not depend on me or you. Before truth is personal, it exists outside of the knower—as a gift. Only once we understand this can we discuss and disagree about its content.

Truth exists outside of us, but it also needs to be personally desired and encountered.

Learning as Participation

Along with the personal nature of learning, you also learn by participating with others. You are not alone on the quest for understanding. In college, you have classmates, teachers, roommates, teammates, staff members, your local church, and family to whom you belong. Alan Jacobs proposes that true belonging is about "a fellowship of people who are not so much like-minded as like-hearted...For there can be more genuine fellowship among those who share the same disposition than among those who share the same beliefs, especially if that is toward kindness and generosity."[8] As you consider friends, it's not important that you think exactly the same way about everything. Rather, it's about belonging to a certain type of people—friends who are generous and charitable interpreters even as you disagree. The question as you look at your fellowship of truth-seekers is whether or not their presence helps you think better, more clearly, and more lovingly. Finding a community of trust in truth-seeking is an important part of college life. These are the people tasked to challenge you and sharpen your thinking, and you have an equal privilege to poke and prod them with your own learning.

As we saw in Chapter 7, when God creates, He gives gifts of Himself. College is about studying the created world—whether that is the physical creation (biology, geology, etc.) or non-physical creation (literature, psychology, history, etc.). The created world that we are invited to study reveals particular and distinct gifts. No created thing can accurately reflect the essence of truth, beauty, and goodness which is God Himself, but each created thing shows an aspect or measure of the Transcendent One. We see the created world with sacramental eyes—through created, ordinary things that points us to the Creator, an extraordinary God.

For anything to exist means that it shares in truth, beauty, and goodness. If something failed to exhibit any semblance of truth, beauty, or goodness, it would cease to exist. It would have no substance to share in reality. When we accurately perceive and discover the God-given gifts in creation, we experience reminders of God. Every created thing shines with hints of God. We learn something about the Giver when we discover the gift given.

Part of our college pilgrimage is to discern where history, people, literature, or science have rightly seen these reminders of God. Since everything remains shot through with grace, the main questions we should be asking are: Where does this reveal truth? Or goodness? Or beauty? In these questions, we seek to participate in the real.

And the college journey also calls us to discern the ways that history, literature, politics, and science have missed reminders of God. So, we ask questions like: Where has history or this historian failed? Where has the scientific discipline overstepped its bounds? What brokenness is psychology attempting to fix? There are ways that each academic subject is disordered that distort these reminders of God. This task of learning is to discern where certain subjects are insubstantial, but the main goal is to commune with the truth—those transcendent realities. When we rightly understand a certain subject, we take our understanding all the way to the Gift Giver. We come to a closer intimacy with the Gift Giver when we rightly discern the gift.

While everything reflects God, some particular things reflect God more than others. For example, humans, made in the image of God, will reflect more of God than turtles. But turtles can still reveal the patience of God by their slow and steady pace. Our ability to perceive this reality in other created subjects is affected by sin. I might not display the fullness of my humanity as a created being because I am not good, act ugly, or suppress the truth. That diminishes my reflection of God. Or, because my desires have been malformed, I may not perceive the beauty of a painting or song. Perhaps I need to mature in order to see this piece of creation more accurately as a reminder of God.

In our studies, the same is true. Some books reflect more light—more truth, beauty, and goodness—than others. Those books with more substance of the real are worthy of effort and time. Sure, it's good to study things that are less true as a comparative exercise but devoting your life to comic books may not reward you—or it will "reward" you in destructive ways. We only have so much time, and we ought to devote our time to what has been passed down to us as most worthy to study.

If all things ultimately find their fullness in relation to God, then that means truth can be discussed and communicated. The universality of truth means it can be comprehended universally—by everyone who seeks the truth. Just as rain falls on the unrighteous and the righteous (Matt. 5:45), so truth can be seen by good people and evil people—and everyone in between. In theological terms, this is called common grace: truth revealed and discoverable to all humanity. Truth is a public good that all can share, as God is not something we master or control. That's part of truth's universality and transferability. That is, whether you are black, and the author is white, or the teacher is a woman, and you are a man, truth is a commonality that binds people together. Participation in truth is not contingent on personality, background, or genetic makeup. Furthermore, because others are different than you, they may see something you did not see and help you more fully become acquainted with the truth. Or because a teacher has experienced something before, they may be able to teach an idea that you did not notice at first glance. In any case, the beauty of learning is that you are a participant.

Whether you participate or not and how well you participate is up to you—like opening or closing your eyes. The truth does not change, but our ability to see it does. God's world of wonder is there, ready to be seen, waiting to change you. All along, truth invites you to belong.

Conclusion

The invitation to learn is a social process. The initial desire for a subject or topic should be attended to. Follow that erotic desire until it gives birth to new desire. It will require commitment and discipline that will reward you with insight and more passion. Love takes you outside of yourself to enter the world of the writer or the perspective of a classmate. Friendships are forged in these uncomfortable spaces where love takes you. An alternative way to live is in indifference. It will ask little of you and you will be changed very little.

But if you let love draw you outside of yourself, the truth you find will be cultivated and corrected in community. You need others to correct your perception as others may need you to correct their understandings. You may need to mature a bit to see the reality of goodness in a subject or beauty in a book. But when you come to that subject a few years later and begin to see the real in it, you will find that the book did not change. You did. This learning process happens best in relationship and relationship requires intimacy. Desire will draw you into closer intimacy with God, to other people, and even academic subjects themselves on your quest for truth.

Discussion Questions

1. In your own words, how is education erotic? Do you think that's true? Why or why not?
2. How is learning social? How does this change the way you journey on your educational path?
3. Describe a book or class that you found truly enjoyable. What made it enjoyable?
4. If education is pursued by desire, what would make you desire learning?
5. Dietrich von Hildebrand once said that there's a difference between the subjectively satisfying and the objectively valuable. What do you think he means?
6. Could you say that reading a certain book is "better" or "worse" for you? Or that someone's taste in music or movies is "better" or "worse"? Why or why not?

Notes

1. St. Augustine, *Confessions,* trans. Henry Chadwick (New York: Oxford University Press, 2008), 13.9.10.

2. Joseph Pieper, *Faith, Hope Love* (San Francisco: Ignatius Press, 1997), 265.

3. Esther Lightcap Meek. *Loving to Know: Introducing Covenant Epistemology* (Eugene, OR: Cascade, 2011), 250.

4. Parker Palmer, *To Know as We Are Known* (San Francisco: Harper & Row, 1983), 31.

5. Michael Polanyi, *Personal Knowledge; Towards a Post-critical Philosophy* (Chicago: University of Chicago Press, 1958), 163).

6. Palmer, *To Know as We Are Known*, 7.

7. Esther Lightcap Meek, *Loving to Know: Introducing Covenantal Epistemology* (Eugene, OR: Cascade, 2011), 32.

8. Alan Jacobs, *How to Think: A Survival Guide for a World at Odds* (New York: Currency, 2017), 62, 69.

CHAPTER 10

Learning as Practice: The Love of Wisdom

"To know wisdom and instruction,
to understand words of insight,
to receive instruction in wise dealing,
in righteousness, justice, and equity;
to give prudence to the simple,
knowledge and discretion to the youth—
Let the wise hear and increase in learning,
and the one who understands obtain guidance,
to understand a proverb and a saying,
the words of the wise and their riddles.
The fear of the LORD is the beginning of knowledge;
fools despise wisdom and instruction."

Proverbs 1:2–7

The word "philosophy" means "love of wisdom." This definition encompasses the main points of this book. College is about a life of love and developing to be a certain type of person—a wise one. We should desire to be people who love wisdom. College is not the only opportunity to grow in loving wisdom, but it does provide unique opportunities to build a proper foundation. These years are about asking and seeking answers to important questions: what is the good life? How do I live into it and nurture it? How do I care for the flourishing life that I find compelling? It's one thing to have a vision of the good life; it's a whole different undertaking to live into that good life. I may have a vision of being a professional piano player, but if I don't know how to play the piano, then my vision only takes me so far. I need practical wisdom on how to arrive at the vision. Knowing is only half the battle. You also must do something about it.

In this chapter, I want to suggest that along with the gift of and participation in truth, we must put what we've learned to practice. If truth sits in your intellect without working its way into your life, it shows that you don't yet really know the truth. If you know the right thing to do but fail to do it, then you don't really know it—at least not in any profound way. Applying the truth that you know is called wisdom.

The Goal of Wisdom in Education

Many institutions no longer have a vocabulary for and purpose of moral formation and wisdom. The good thing about a Christian college is that no part of your life is off limits from discussion, cultivation, and formation. A public education might not talk about your spiritual or moral life, but here at the Christian liberal arts college, that's kind of our deal. We have the resources of faith to discuss character, virtue, and the good life.

A robust Christian liberal arts education provides formation for wisdom. As we have seen, the world is full of information. Libraries are overflowing with books. Techniques and skills are constantly changing. What the world needs—even what the job market needs—are those who are wise. The world needs people who display and act with wisdom. Wisdom requires seeing the interconnectedness of knowledge and the choices we make to decisively act in each situation. Knowledge, awareness of context, and virtuous character are all necessary for a person marked by wisdom.

I know you're anxious about choosing and getting a job. This college thing costs a lot of money that needs to be paid somehow. I get it. But more important than what you learn or the skills you acquire in college is what kind of person you are and are becoming. The goal of a Christian liberal arts college is to give you a foundation to become a wise person. Being wise is about living a well-ordered life.

Wisdom will benefit you in whatever job you pursue. Further, most people will change jobs four times in their first years of employment.[1] A recent study suggests that the new workplace will force employees to change careers (not jobs within the same field) eight times.[2] Typically, your grandparents started in a field and finished in that same field, even if they moved or made a parallel job switch. But as folk musician Bob Dylan sang, "The Times, They are A-Changin." Our technological age and the increasing move to automation may only enhance this trend. Your major may not even be needed in twenty years. Some argue that higher education needs to be made shorter and more geared toward job skills because there will be a wave of continuing education or re-education with shifts in the job market. Why devote these four years to a career that may not exist in twenty years?

However, another way forward is by going back to the ancient past. Perhaps what you need is not more narrow skills but broader ones. Carol Quinn in the *Washington Times* suggests:

> Today's graduates need broadly transferable skills—
> how to communicate, build a team in a multicultur-
> al work environment, tackle an intractable problem,
> analyze complex data and make timely decisions with
> imperfect information. Similarly, graduates need the
> work ethic and resilience to learn new fields quickly,
> so that they can recognize and adjust to unpredictable
> shifts in our global economy and world. And to lead
> in a pluralistic, free society, they need deeply rooted
> humane instincts: compassion, intellectual curiosity,
> self-awareness, integrity and moral courage. These are
> not circumscribed technical skills. These are charac-
> ter attributes and habits of mind that will enable our
> nation's children to think critically, communicate clear-
> ly, and design ethical, sustainable solutions to societal
> challenges we cannot yet imagine.[3]

In other words, Quinn affirms the goal of a liberal arts education: graduates need wisdom, or applied knowledge. They need the habits of life that will lead to being compassionate and intellectually curious. These are goods whether or not they "pay off" in a good job. Quinn points out, though, that these character traits often do pay off in good jobs.

In an increasingly technological age, we need students alive to their own and others' humanity. In a *New York Times* article, David Brooks reported on a community school for foster children in Italy called "Cometa."[4] The school picks up on themes of personhood and humanity that employers want. The people of Cometa believe beauty educates. With this fundamental belief, they desire to show hospitality. While most machines are focused around completing physical tasks, Brooks explains, "No machine will be able to create the feeling of a loving home. Whether they are being trained as waiters, carpenters, fabric designers or pastry chefs, students are taught to understand and create hospitable experiences. 'Everything is a home,' said Mele. 'Everything says, "Welcome to my home."'[5] This beautiful vision of education, even in the trades, can be cultivated on every educational campus, in every classroom, and through any task. A machine can't show hospitality or love. It can't be a person because that's exactly what it is not. Love is what makes the world go around and the life-giving feature of the universe. People with wisdom can pursue their careers with hospitality and with human connection.

Interconnectedness of Knowledge

As lovers pointed toward God, Christians have a coherent story and understanding of the good, the true, and the beautiful. Without a clear tradition or guiding principles, the university becomes subject to what sells and what works. Since human beings exist as holistic creatures, they need a holistic education—one that touches not only cognition but also the affections.

Our modern culture fragments this unified pursuit. Historically, the educational discipline of science, art, and ethics corresponded with truth, beauty, and goodness respectively. However, as was noted in the first half of this book, there was a growing tendency to specialize. Rather than seeing these disciplines as a gift from God that are unified in Him, they battled with one another for supreme emphasis in a university.

Universities, Christian or not, tend to specialize in truth. However, for the next generation of Christian witness in the West, we will need young people prepared to promote and defend the good and the beautiful, as well. In a culture that denies truth, a full Christian witness and

education encompass the involvement of beauty and goodness. People may not be persuaded of the Christian testi-
mony rationally, but people of character that the church
forms and the art the church produces will be compelling
witnesses to the world. Since a human is not just a "brain
on a stick," you need formation that engages your heart.
You need a compelling picture of the good. You need to
feel the beauty of Christianity in your bones more than
consider it in your head.

The Christian college has the resources for this holistic
emphasis in every subject. I want you to be involved in the
college in such a way that you are captivated by a vision for a
good life, not merely given options. You already have options,
tons of options. The issue is discerning which option to take.
Wisdom knows which option to take in each circumstance,
and part of seeing the circumstance is seeing the full picture
from different perspectives. Part of your development here is
developing wisdom, and being around wise guides, to help
you know the best way to travel.

Education as Craft

This type of education which emphasizes wisdom is something like a craft or a skill. It is not a mechanical or scientific
process but an artistic one. Just like making art, education
requires contact with reality.

Artists come to be intimately acquainted with their craft
in a similar way an athlete falls in love with a game. They both
come to know their medium through time and intention. A
painter or sculptor knows what clay can do and what it can't
do in the same way a basketball player knows what moves
work in a specific situation and what will result in a turnover.
They know its limits. Knowledge and skill lead to a certain
respect for the material or craft. Consequently, both trained

artist and athlete will innovate in distinct ways because they dedicate their lives to their craft.

I could tell you what clay is like, but unless you hold it in your hands, spin it on a lathe, and work it between your fingers, you won't know what its exact properties are or what its nature is. I could tell you how to swing a baseball bat, but unless you hold one in your hands and see what a pitch coming at you feels like, you won't be a baseball player. I could tell you all about a subject, discipline, or vocation, but unless you enter it, receive it as gift, and develop your talent, you won't be very successful.

Knowledge leads to skill, and skill needs practice. At first, you may struggle to make a basketball shot or shape a bowl. Even when you do, it will be imperfect and awkward. Yet with practice, you acquire a skill. You learn how to excel through habits and, after a while, it almost becomes natural—like putting on a t-shirt or walking to class. You don't think about the activity—it has become second nature.

Education is pursued in the same way: as a practice that we gradually improve. Craft needs contact with the real world, just as knowing has to come from encounters in the real world. Craft is a dialogue between artist and material just as education is a dialogue between subject and student. Craft is rooted in love of a material, just as education is rooted in love of a subject. Education, in other words, is a craft.

God created us as image bearers, and that also means that He made us creative. Without exercising creativity, we are causing destruction to the world and to our very selves. The best creators are learners. The best way to learn is through two things: loving attentiveness to the world and mentorship. We must come to love a subject, pay attention to it, be mentored in it, respect it, and in so doing, add to it.

Loving Attentiveness

One of the hard things in the modern world is paying attention. Almost every aspect of modern life assists in distracting you. In your pocket (assuming some sort of smartphone is in your pocket) the whole world awaits. You can text a friend, snap a picture, search for the answer to a question, or just scroll in boredom. In how the world portrays modern life, the worst thing you can be is bored. Yet there are whole industries whose aim is to keep you distracted. In fact, I imagine that it may be difficult for you to pay attention without checking your phone as you read a single page of this book.

Here's an unfortunate truth, though: to be great at anything requires the dedication of attention. If you want to be a great artist, you need to be dedicated to the craft of painting or drawing. If you want to be a great baseball player, you need to love the craft enough to devote time to it. If you brought your phone or television with you to a practice, just in case things get boring, I'm guessing a coach would not respond in the positive.

In the same way, education requires loving attention. Cal Newport observes, "Our brains instead construct our world-view based on *what we pay attention to*...As Gallagher summarizes: 'Who you are, what you think, feel, and do, what you love—is the sum of what you focus on.'"[6] Historically, the liberal arts were heralded as a training ground for what to pay attention to. If you remember David Foster Wallace's commencement speech in Chapter 6, he perceives that most people, including himself, pay attention to themselves to the exclusion of everyone else. This attentiveness to self is most people's default setting, hard-wired into one's brain. He continues to the purpose of a liberal arts education: not learning what to think but "learning how to exercise some control over how and what you think. It means being conscious and aware enough to choose what you pay attention to and to choose how you construct meaning from experience."[7] Wallace gives the example of going to the supermarket in a routine, frustrating way after a long day at work. There at the long check-out line with inconsiderate people or on the drive home when a Hummer cuts him off, there is a choice of interpretation and awareness. At that moment, the person can choose to think charitably about the situation or frame their existence around themselves. He argues that the liberal arts have "almost nothing to do with knowledge and everything to do with simple awareness."[8] To focus on what to pay attention to is one of the main goals of a Christian liberal arts education.

While selfishness shrinks our attention, love enlarges our attention to include other people and other subjects. The initial attraction may not be natural, but love pulls us out of ourselves and disposes us toward attending beyond immediate appreciation or enjoyment. In essence, love leads the student outside of oneself to be attentive to another. Love draws the student to something alien, and education happens when attention to something outside of oneself is rewarded. Education, if you remember, is about expanding your loves, and attentiveness is a key factor in this expansion.

In the same vein, Simone Weil draws out the implication of attention to tough or unenjoyable subjects. Wrestling with a difficult subject, or even a subject one is prone to dislike, is a means of forming attention. She explains, "The key to a Christian conception of studies is the realization that prayer consists of attention."[9] Here, Weil points out that the key to and purpose of study is attention. Studying subjects prime the knower for higher attention and contemplation. She uses the example of geometry. Even if someone wrestles for an hour and does not arrive at the correct conclusion, that person is formed in the attention necessary in seeking God.

Perhaps educational institutions are too quick to give easy, pat answers in an effort to relieve sitting with discomfort. But the quest for truth requires struggle. If students don't struggle, then it diminishes their ability to pay attention to God in the post-college years. Struggle requires attention.

To summarize, Alan Jacobs may be helpful: "Attentiveness is an ethical as well as an intellectual matter; it's about treating our neighbors as they deserve as much as it's about getting the right facts into our heads."[10] Being certain kinds of people that model Christlikeness requires that we treat others as they deserve—and those others start with those in your dorm hall or classroom and include the people who wrote your textbooks.

Something I have seen in recent years is the emergence of students wearing AirPods or headphones in class. Now, maybe they think I'm too far away to notice, or their tiny earbuds are hidden behind a hoodie, or perhaps they know I see them and simply don't think I care. Regardless, this small act of presentation is a moral decision. Now, I don't necessarily care about a particular student hearing about whatever I am waxing eloquently about (Though I'm sure it's life-changing, and they're missing out, but that's beside the point). In other words, the use of cell phones or earbuds in class communicates to me a matter beyond what information they are missing. They say: "You are boring. I'd rather tune you out. You are not important." Now all those things may be true, but they are ethical postures. You are treating a living human being as disposable based on how interesting he or she is, and you will go on to give others worth based on what they can do for you. Care and respect are more important to me than whatever I may be lecturing about on a given day. Often, how we treat one another well starts with attention. And if we can do that in the classroom, then maybe we will deal with boring or uninteresting people with love when we encounter them in the world. And maybe, just maybe, we will learn that even they have something to teach us.

Mentoring

When he was in school, the children's television host Mister Rogers once recalled a time that he observed children. He was training under the child psychologist, Margaret McFarland. Dr. McFarland had a sculptor come in to teach the children about pottery. Here is what she told the sculptor: "I don't want you to teach sculpting. I want you simply to sit with the children and do what you feel you'd like to with the clay." Fred recalls, "Well, the kids started using clay—that medium—in the most wonderful ways. And that wouldn't have happened if this gifted sculptor hadn't loved clay right in front of them." This led Mister Rogers to a fitting definition of the best teaching: "They just love what they're doing, and love it in front of others."[11] I think you will find this is true: even the subjects you find most boring can be made enjoyable by a teacher who loves their subject—like a master craftsman who loves their material. Teaching is not just a matter of transferring information but of loving your subject.

Faculty are not only important for your intellectual or economic success—moral formation requires moral exemplars. As you pick a college, you are also picking a faculty, and hopefully, a group of mentors. In essence, you are saying, "I think I want to be like these people at the end of four years—these graduates and these teacher-mentors." We learn virtue, the certain type of person we want to be, through imitation. How a faculty member treats an elementary question, a hot topic, or a struggling student will suggest how you should handle the same. The classroom is like an orchestra. The habits and tone of a classroom will affect your understanding of how exactly to play your part, how to listen, when to participate, and when to refrain. There is a sense in which the passion and interest a scholar takes in his field can function by a kind of osmosis to his or her students. Like the sculptor in Mister Rogers neighborhood, some teachers will ignite a passion for a subject that you thought you had no interest in.

A good faculty member can be a master for the life of flourishing. Both Augustine and Steven Garber propose the significance of mentoring. Augustine is worth quoting at length on the role of teacher:

> What I would like to know is whether you possess and can accurately impart to others anything supremely important and wholesome. It's ridiculous if, after you've learned a lot of unnecessary things in order to prepare people to listen to you tell them what is indispensable, you yourself don't possess it; and if, while you are busy learning how to get their attention, you refuse to learn what to teach them when you've gained it. But if you say that you already know, and answer that it's Christian doctrine (I know that you prefer this to everything else and entrust your hope of eternal salvation to this alone), you don't need to be familiar with the dialogues of Cicero and a collection of the beggarly and divided opinions of other people to win an audience. *Attract them by your way of life if you want them to receive such a teaching from you.*[12]

On this passage, Garber casts a vision for what learning is all about: "...teachers opening their lives to students, allowing an apprenticeship in what is *supremely important.*"[13] Find those teachers you want to be like. Take their classes. Go to them during their office hours. Ask them questions. Be mentored by them. That's why we are here.

Conclusion

Matthew Crawford, who holds a doctorate in philosophy and runs a motorcycle repair shop, is one other author who recommends education as a sort of craft. In *The World Beyond Your Head,* he uses the example of a pipe organ.[14] To be a master craftsman of a pipe organ requires one to be initiated into the craft, which requires attention, concentration, and perception. It is insufficient to merely know the history or function of the pipe organ; it requires a critical engagement with the design and method of the past combined with an orientation toward the future. For example, traditional organs require a wood chip in the pipe, but wood decays quickly and easily. An innovation was making this piece from metal rather than wood. To be a master craftsman, one must be initiated into the tradition to carry it forward, and this initiation can only be done by someone within the trade who trains an apprentice to be a conversation partner. Thus, craftsmanship involves a deep dive into a particular emphasis as well as a working knowledge of how their piece fits into the bigger picture—the connectedness of their particular knowledge. It is specialized within a generalized framework—like a major within a liberal arts foundation. It seems modern education has lost the skill of learning and living well, so schools often settle for a counterfeit. Education has become accustomed to the cheap and easy and has lost the craft of sustaining education through the generations—one that requires attentiveness and mentoring.

Discussion Questions

1. Earlier, I asked you to identify the 5 most famous people in America. Who are the two most important people you respect? What makes them different from famous people?
   a. If you want to be more like the people you respect, how do you do that?
   b. How do you find good teachers and mentors?
2. How is wisdom different from knowledge?
3. How is education like a craft?
4. If education requires attention, what are impediments to your attention in the classroom?

Notes

1. Guy Berger, "Will This Year's College Grads Job-Hop More than Previous Grads?" *LinkedIn*, April 12, 2016, https://blog.linkedin.com/2016/04/12/will-this-year_s-college-grads-job-hop-more-than-previous-grads.

2. Noted in Tim Clydesdale, *The Purposeful Graduate Why Colleges Must Talk to Students about Vocation* (Chicago: University of Chicago, 2015), 109.

3. Carol Quinn, "Liberal Education in the Age of Trump," *The Washington Post*, December 30, 2016, https://www.washingtonpost.com/news/grade-point/wp/2016/12/30/liberal-arts-education-in-the-age-of-trump/?utm_term=.f38051d5aded.

4. David Brooks, "The Loving Place for Children That Assumes Hospitality," *The New York Times*. April 30, 2018, accessed April 30, 2018, https://www.nytimes.com/2018/04/30/opinion/loving-children-com-eta-italy.html.

5. Ibid.

6. Cal Newport, *Deep Work: Rules for Focused Success in a Distracted World* (New York: Grand Central Publishing, 2016), 77, emphasis original.

7. David Foster Wallace, "This Is Water," Commencement Address at Kenyon College, accessed August 11, 2018, https://web.ics.purdue.edu/~drkelly/DFWKenyonAddress2005.pdf.

8. Ibid.

9. Simone Weil, *Waiting on God* (New York: Harper Perennial Modern Classics, 2009), 57.

10. Alan Jacobs, "How to Read a Book," in *Liberal Arts for the Christian Life,* ed. Jeffrey Davis and Philip Ryken (Wheaton, IL: Crossway, 2012), 127.

11. This is story is documented in Shea Tuttle, *Exactly as You Are: The Life and Faith of Mister Rogers* (Grand Rapids: Eerdmans Press, 2019), 62.

12. John Leinenweber, *The Letters of Saint Augustine* (Liguori, MO: Triumph Books, 1992), 99, emphasis added.

13. Steven Garber, *The Fabric of Faithfulness: Common Grace for the Common Good* (Downers Grove, IL: InterVarsity Press, 2014), 151.

14. Matthew Crawford, *The World Beyond Your Head: On Becoming an Individual in an Age of Distraction* (New York: Farrar, Straus and Giroux, 2015).

CHAPTER 11

Learning in Community: Learning to Love Broken Places

"It is very much in the gift of community to enrich individual lives, and it is the gift of any individual to enrich the community."

Marilynne Robinson, *When I Was a Child, I Read Books*

Imagine yourself as a high school freshman. If you were like me, you were a scrawny, pimple-faced, immature little person. You were scared yet excited—fearful yet hopeful. For four years, you suffered through classes, maybe did some extracurricular activities—plays or band or sports—and you matured. Perhaps you experienced love, perhaps heartbreak. But at the end of those four years of high school, you realized that you are not the same person. Physically and emotionally, you changed.

In many ways, this will be your experience in college. Just as you find it hard to recognize that fourteen-year-old who was you at the end of high school, so at the end of the college years, it may be difficult to recognize that eighteen-year-old you. These college years from eighteen to twenty-two are formative for everyone—whether they choose college or not. You are out on your own, away from parental supervision, and in many ways you get to choose the person you want to be. You have decided to devote these formative years to a particular college.

Up to this last chapter, I've devoted a lot of discussion to what goes on inside the college classroom, because I think the classroom is the unique place where formation happens on a college campus. If not, it's one expensive vacation (that you will pay for later). But I also recognize that so much of your college experience happens outside the classroom—most likely, it's in your residence hall, in chapel or an on-campus Bible study, forming new friendships in the student center or coffee shop, or at a sports arena watching or playing a game. You don't spend all your time in the classroom or doing homework. As Alison Gopnik likes to remind her students, "If you've never at some point stayed up all night talking to your new boyfriend about the meaning of life instead of preparing for the test, then you're not really an intellectual."[1] Be curious and experience what college life has to offer. Pursue the things that matter—that may mean not getting an A+ on a particular test. It's okay. You'll survive.

The college you have chosen will influence you over the next four years. Your experience will cultivate some vision of the good life. What really matters to a college boils down to what it does. Author and philosopher James KA Smith calls these habits of place "cultural liturgies."[2] The "liturgy" literally means "the work of the people"—every church service has a liturgy or the way they do things in worship.

Maybe it's a more formal liturgy, maybe it's just three songs, a prayer, and a sermon. But these practices are important, and they tell a story. Smith applies this religious term to cultural practices. Whether we like it or not, the practices we participate in are not neutral; they do something to us. Smith uses the example of a state school. No one there will give you a pamphlet to define what really matters or their educational philosophy. But what truly matters hides within the college's practices. Typically, the practice of a big state school is this: endure classes during the week. Show up or not—it doesn't matter much. The good life is experienced on the weekends with "darties" (day parties) that lead to the big event on the college campus: the football game. Emotions ride or fall on how the team does. Campus life is impacted by excitement or despair. This "liturgy" will form you to work for the weekend, when real life happens—centered around your alma mater's fall schedule.

Again, no one will come up and tell you, "This is what matters at our school." What matters is more hidden, underneath the practices of the place. The college you have chosen will give you a vision of the good life shaped by their habits. These habits are formative and are experienced (mostly) outside the college classroom.

Being Formed in a Place

You are made by layers of formative influences. You are not an autonomous individual making decisions for yourself. You see from a place. As much as modern culture may promote individuality, you are a product of your environment in real and important ways. For instance, your body has an impact on how you view the world. Obviously, your family and community affect you in profound ways. These formative influences shape how you imagine the world.

Embodied Existence

You live in this hunk of flesh called a body. You have physical eyes that see and a physical tongue that tastes. God made your body good and gifted it with these abilities. How you treat your body affects other aspects of existence. Things like diet, exercise, and sleep have formative influences on how you think, respond, and make decisions. As such, care ought to be given to how you treat your body because your body will have an impact on how you experience the classroom. Staying up late at night will impact class the next day. Exercise has been shown to increase creativity and decrease stress. Caring for your body is part of what it means to cultivate and steward what God has given you.

Bodies are not some evil containers for a pure soul. Your body matters. You experience the world in a body. If you are a woman rather than a man, then your experience will be different. If you are black rather than white, your embodied experience will be different. I remember seeing a tweet from one of my African American friends a few years ago. He was looking for an alternative work-out to running because he thought running would make him look suspicious as a black man. I thought, "Come on. Just go for a run." Then Ahmaud Arbery was shot in a neighborhood for looking "suspicious" on a run, and I realized I needed to repent. I thought I knew more about the black experience than my black friend. The same principle applies to women running. As a white man, I've never left my house for a run and felt scared that I may be accosted or look suspicious. But minorities and females consider these things that I never have to think about. As much as I want to say that someone different from me won't experience the classroom differently because it's a place of equity, the reality is that each person probably will. And we all need to make note of it. Living in a system as a man or woman, Asian or Hispanic, can alter how a person processes reality. Again, whether I like it or not, it's the truth.

This reality is one reason why diversity is so important in education. By another's embodied existence, each person, in their own skin, provides alternative perspectives, especially those of minority cultures. The idea of embodiment recognizes that people see from somewhere. We need multiple perspectives to see clearly. As a student, you add something to the class in your "somewhere-ness"—whether that be a small farming community or an elite prep school. These dynamics matter, because bodies matter, and a knower knows from a location and perspective. The location brings with it biases good and bad, but nevertheless real.

Forged in Community

St. Augustine defines a people as "a gathered multitude of rational beings united by agreeing to share the things they love."[3] A college is a people with common loves. We saw that in the first half of the book: do colleges love intellect most? Or job skills? Or social causes? Or sports? Whatever they love binds them together and defines them.

You have chosen a college. Whether you like it or not, you will be formed by the community you have chosen and the things they love. Ideally, you have chosen a place with people that you want to be like—to be a certain type of person in the identity to which you aspire. That's the power of community.

The most basic form of community is the family. Your family has influenced you in an abundance of ways. They impact some of you in large ways: your identity, story, and purpose. They affect most of you in small ways: how you spend money or the "right" way to argue. They may have taught you what or who to worship, and you react to your upbringing by either owning it or shunning it. But your family provides the building blocks by which you interpret the world. They have and will influence what you pay attention to, what matters most, and what you make of what you see.

The same thing happens at the communal level. What is true of the family is true of these new friends around you in college. A community shapes how you will imagine the story in which you find yourself. This story helps a person make sense of life. Alasdair MacIntyre writes, "The story of my life is always embedded in the story of those communities from which I derive my identity...What I am, therefore, is what I inherit, a specific past that is present to some degree in my present."[4] The story grounds the "why" of living, and you do not create it. You inherit it from your community.

Borrowing an environmental term, David Brooks calls this communal dimension of formation a "moral ecology." He defines it as

> a set of norms, assumptions, beliefs, and habits of be-havior and an institutionalized set of moral demands that emerge organically. Our moral ecology encourages us to be a certain sort of person...The moral ecology of a given moment is never unanimous; there are always rebels, critics, and outsiders. But each moral climate is a collective response to the problems of the moment and it shapes the people who live in it.[5]

Just as plants thrive in a certain "ecology" or "environment," so you as a human find certain norms or assumptions in which you "plant" yourself to "grow." How do you relate to others? How are they influencing you, and you them? A community—whether a nation, a city, or a college—influences you. Even if you react against the normal "ecology" of a place, that particular place still forms you in what you are reacting against. As part of campus life, you will be drawn to certain ways of seeing and being in the world—a certain story of the world. You will need to reflect on and consider what story the campus life is telling you, how it shapes you, and who you want to be in light of these realities.

What's Normal?: A Cultural Imagination

Your embodied existence and the community you are in will form you to love in certain directions. In some ways, you can choose to opt-in. Will you hang out with the athletes, and which ones? Or will you choose the outdoor group and be formed to love nature, rock climbing, and hiking? Your campus life does not require you to love what it loves, but your choices and habits will form you to love *something*. In many ways, you get to choose what to love, which will direct who you will be.

The communal formation has a direct impact on how you imagine the world. By imagine, I do not mean some childish "imagination"—like playing dress up or with dolls. Imagination is similar to what you think is normal. Richard Sibbes, an early Puritan pastor defined imagination as "a power of the soul" which is "bordering between our senses and our understanding."[6] Imagination is the disposition with which we approach the world. It provides an interpretive framework of what we see. In many ways, imagination is what we find believable or persuasive. Perception is not a passive process by which we neutrally see the world. Experience, family, and society train a person to imagine the world in a certain way.

Our imagination is affected by the cultural norms and habits of a place. A child growing up in poverty will function from a different set of assumptions about the world than someone born into wealth. A person raised in a southern rural community will likely view the world slightly differently than someone raised in the Pacific Northwest. A black woman will likely see and imagine the world differently than a Hispanic man. These different assumptions are given, not chosen. In other words, our imagination is unconscious. Think back to David Foster Wallace's joke about fish in water. The goal is to grow in our awareness of how we see the world, which means listening to how other people see the world. By so doing, we can get a better sense of what our "water" is with its certain limitations and advantages.

Speaking Back to Place

With all these formative influences recognized and affirmed, the heart is responsible and able to respond. Things around you may entice you, but they do not control you. The Bible constantly points to the heart, or soul, as the morally responsible center. Your institution can certainly hold sway over you and guide your intuitions in a certain direction, but it does not bind you to a definitive path. The heart gives us moral responsibility to distinguish, evaluate, and contribute to a moral ecology.

As responsible agents capable of change, David Brooks suggests that we can speak back to how we've been formed. We get to choose the story we tell about our lives. He writes,

> We're born into cultures, nations, and languages that we didn't choose. We're born with certain brain chemicals and genetic predispositions that we can't control. We're sometimes thrust into social conditions that we detest. But among all the things we don't control, we do have some control over our stories. We do have a conscious say in selecting the narrative we will use to organize perceptions.[7]

Reflection allows a person to re-imagine the ordinary. It allows a pause, to recognize the story one finds themselves in and change. Pausing to evaluate can also increase appreciation for the habits in which one regularly participates.

What does all this mean for your time as an undergraduate? As much as you will be formed by your institution, you are also a member of your institution. In many ways, you get to influence campus life as you will be affected by campus life. You get to contribute to the "moral ecology" of campus life. Oftentimes, we feel like we're helpless to make a change—that we're on this roller coaster of campus life that we have no control over. In some ways, that is true. Community has powerful influence. But you also have a call, an opportunity, even an obligation, to enrich campus life by your participation in it.

With this holistic understanding of formation, I hope you see that education is about the whole person—not merely mental formation. So often, Christianity, and perhaps especially Christian education, reduces itself to learning a different doctrine or better belief system. But Christianity and the sort of Christian education that you will get at a Christian liberal arts college is an invitation to an alternative way of life.

On the one hand, you are formed by the college you choose to attend. Friends, faculty members, staff, and coaches will all impact your view of the world. They will shape your "imagination" and what you think is "normal." It's important to recognize that you *have* a "normal" and how other imaginations can broaden how you understand your normal. On the other hand, you are not subject to your friends, faculty members, staff, and coaches. They will influence you, but you will also influence them. You are a part of a community, and as a member of this community, your participation matters. You are a shaper of campus culture—for good or for ill.

Conclusion

On January 6, 2021, a group of individuals stormed the U.S. Capitol in defiance of the election results. I remember turning the television on and seeing fellow Americans break into our governmental headquarters and ransack it. Seeing the events in real-time was surreal. I imagined things like this happeneing in developing countries with unstable political systems but not here. Not in America. Not in my country.

The people who charged the Capitol building imagined themselves as patriots who loved their country and wanted to rescue America. The riot sparked a conversation over the next few weeks on what it means to be a patriot. What does it mean to love your country?

At the same time, I had planned to discuss a chapter in class by the Catholic writer G.K. Chesterton. It's a chapter called "Flag of the World" in his well-known book titled *Orthodoxy*. In the chapter, he wrestles with what it means to be born in and belong to a place. He writes, "A man belongs to this world before he begins to ask if it is nice to belong to it."[8]

In the same way, you belong to your college now, before you begin to ask if it is nice to belong to it. There will be plenty of time over the four years to ask that question: is it nice to belong here? But you do—in the same way you belong to America. There is part of the process of education when you ask that question. Can you still love your college when you find out they denied entrance to women or minorities at some point? Or, when your friend gets expelled for what you deem a minor infraction? Is it still nice to belong?

Even before you ask those questions, you belong. What makes a certain place great is not its history or lack of injustice. What makes a place great, as Chesterton argues, are those who love it. He says of the historic Roman Empire, "Men did not love Rome because she was great. She was great because they loved her."[9] There is one way to be a patriot that says, "There is nothing wrong with this place. It's awesome! We need loyalty." And there's another way to be a patriot that says, "We need to critique this place because it's not truly great. We need honesty." Chesterton recommends a third way to love your place: to love it even as you see its brokenness. And isn't that how we love anything? We are committed to something; we are loyal to it—despite its flaws. We don't ignore certain faults, but we love a person or place through their flaws—like in a marriage.

During your time in college, there will be staff members who may mistreat you. Administrators may make unjust decisions. Professors may not be as gracious as you hope. Roommates will be annoying. What do you do then? What do you do when the place that you belong turns out to not be as nice as you'd hoped? One way is to ignore it. "Who cares? They are a marginal few, and this place rules." The other way is to critique everything. "These people stink, this place stinks, and I hate it. I'm leaving." But being a true patriot of a place, a good member of a place, is to stare open-eyed at its brokenness. If you do not yet know how it is broken, just give it time. Every place is.

But with the same intensity, we commit to love our place—which may mean we need to critique it. We may need to speak truth to power and fix the broken things. Even as we criticize though, we love. If we did not love it, we would be indifferent to the ills and brokenness. Indifference is no way to live. College is a training ground in learning to love a broken yet beautiful world.

Discussion Questions

1. Describe the place you are from. What's it like? If you were to take a classmate there, how would you spend your day?
2. Describe your family. How do you think they have shaped you as you start college?
3. What are some of your favorite parts about your college? What are some of your least favorite parts?
4. How do you think you can contribute to your campus culture? Is there any area you can help improve?

Notes

1. Kate Fillion, "In conversation: Alison Gopnik," *Maclean's*. November 1, 2006, https://www.macleans.ca/general/whats-wrong-with-the-way-we-teach-and-how-a-year-out-of-university-changed-her-sons-life/

2. James KA Smith, *Desiring the Kingdom: Worship, Worldview, and Cultural Formation* (Grand Rapids: Baker Academic, 2009).

3. Oliver O'Donavon, *Common Objects of Love: Moral Reflection and the Shaping of Community* (Grand Rapids: Eerdmans, 2009), 21.

4. Alasdair MacIntyre, *After Virtue: A Study in Moral Theory* (Notre Dame, IN: University of Notre Dame Press, 2007), 221.

5. David Brooks, *The Road to Character* (New York: Random House, 2016), 261.

6. Richard Sibbes, "The Soul's Conflict with Itself, and Victory over Itself by Faith," in *Works of Richard Sibbes*, Vol. 1 ed. Alexander Balloch Grosart (Edinburgh: Banner of Truth Trust, 2001), 178-180.

7. David Brooks, *The Social Animal* (New York: Random House, 2012), 291.

8. GK Chesterton, *Orthodoxy* (Mineola, NY: Dover Publications, 2020), 65.

9. Ibid., 66.

CONCLUSION

Learning to Commit:
An Exercise of Love

"The one thing [Christ] condemns utterly is avoiding the choice. To choose is to commit yourself, and to commit yourself is to run the risk: the risk of failure, the risk of sin, the risk of betrayal. But Jesus can deal with all of these. Forgiveness he never denies us. The man who makes a mistake can repent. But the man who hesitates, who does nothing, who buries his talent in the earth with him, with him he can do nothing."

Fr. Qunitana in *To the Wonder*

"It is also good to love: because love is difficult. For one human being to love another human being: that is perhaps the most difficult task that has been entrusted to us, the ultimate task, the final test and proof, the work for which all other work is merely preparation. That is why young people, who are beginners in everything, are not yet capable of love: it is something they must learn. With their whole being, with all their forces, gathered around their solitary, anxious, upward-beating heart, they must learn to love."

Rainer Marie Rilke, *Letters to a Young Poet*

I have a major aversion to missing out. FOMO is the common diagnosis: Fear of Missing Out. When my friends are somewhere and I am not in that place, it drives me crazy. I hate leaving a party early because I might miss something. Am I the only one?

I'm hindered when I commit. If I have a previous commitment, I may miss out on something "better." So, I like to keep my options open in case something else comes along. In competing choices, choosing to commit can be paralyzing. I'll just not say yes to anything and show up if every other option falls through.

Six years after David Foster Wallace gave his commencement speech at Kenyon College, another novelist took the stage. He was a friend of Wallace. His name was Jonathan Franzen, and he developed this distinction between liking and loving.[1] Liking requires no attachment or commitment. I can like pizza or an acquaintance, and it gives me a certain type of strong affection, but my life is no way different by their presence or absence (but I would miss pizza…). When I like something, I decide that if it pleases me, it can remain, but when it fails to make me happy, I dismiss it. Franzen argues that we live in a "liking world" drawing on the social media reality of "liking posts" translating to how we live in the actual world.

Love is different than liking. Love is the language of commitment and belonging. Love draws us outside of ourselves to another. Other people make some demands on us. Love hurts because it stretches us to identify, in some way, with another's joys and pain. Love decenters my own self and story, while it grows a concern for another's self and story. While liking is easy, love is demanding.

There are all sorts of reasons why commitments are hard. If you, like me, come from a divorced family, then the idea of commitment to one person for a lifetime seems frightening. You've seen a central commitment fail, so better to keep your options open. Or, in the college context, you must commit to a major for these four years, which will make an impact on the rest of your life. That can be scary. What if you commit to a philosophy or faith but then realize you were wrong? What happens then when your foundation shifts? These college years are anxious times where commitments seem to restrict your freedom, where one decision will lead to you missing out on another. It may cause your hands to sweat and your heart to pound a little quicker. Commitments are difficult because they bind you to something. But commitments are also acts of love. And love is what education is for.

Making Commitments

The Catholic theologian and author G. K. Chesterton writes, "The object of opening the mind, as of opening the mouth, is to shut it again on something solid."[2] Openness is crucial for the undergraduate years. You ought to experience and wonder and try new things. However, the goal is not constant speculation and openness forever—if that were even possible. Someone eating with their mouth open the whole time is as equally as gross as they are unproductive. The goal, as Chesterton suggests, is to shut the mouth on something solid; in short, to commit. Especially in these years often marked with uncertainty, angst, and confusion, the undergraduate experience ought to prepare you, as a student, to be devoted to some core commitments.

As we saw in the last chapter, the heart is the center of ultimate commitments. Humanity is not born free: people are born to worship and obey. As such, a liberal education is not meant to free a person to do whatever he or she wants. An education that liberates is one that allows a person to pursue the best commitments. The author David Brooks defines maturity as the realization that "the things you chain yourself to set you free."[3] I love that definition of maturity.

Maturity lies in your ability to make commitments—knowing that your commitments, rather than limiting freedom, actually increase your freedom. For example, I love my wife. To love my wife means I limit myself. I choose to love this woman, Lauren, and not any other. My freedom is limited. However, by limiting my love, I have the freedom to pursue a good and healthy relationship with my wife. If I did not have such limits, my marriage would fall apart. Love is about making the right commitments, and in so doing, sets you free to live a good life.

Jesus says, "If you continue in my word, you are truly my disciples, and you will know the truth, and the truth will set you free" (John 8:31). Referring to this passage, educator Parker Palmer writes, "The idea that freedom is achieved through obedience to truth is also at the heart of liberal education, whose aim is to liberate us through knowledge."[4] As such, the university encourages a certain set of commitments—stated or unstated. It's not about if a graduate chooses to obey or worship, it is a matter of if the graduate will choose rightly, wisely, or virtuously toward the ultimate good. Character, after all, is essentially about commitment. Character is about faithfulness and steadiness over time. To know truth means to intimately interact with it and to follow it with one's whole existence. Which cares will you commit to?

Pastor Tim Keller claims that young adults have always asked at least four such big questions: Who am I? (looking inward); What's the point or meaning of things? (looking outward); Whom should I be with and love? (looking sideways); and in light of the first three answers, What should I do with my life? (looking forward).[5] The good news about choosing a Christian liberal arts college is that Christianity provides coherent answers to these questions. We cannot prescribe what you should do with your life based on those answers, but we can provide a solid foundation on which to build your life.

As a college student, I hope you're searching for something worth believing in—something worth committing to. If the college does not provide a coherent set of answers, then you are left to your own unfettered devices. It would be equivalent to allowing a child to learn about sex from their ten-year-old friend rather than a wise guide who can instruct them on their path. The faculty and staff will not make you commit to a certain way of life, but you will find experienced navigators who provide meaningful feedback to the questions you have. So, as you ask questions, explore different answers.

Along the same line as Keller, David Brooks spoke to Dartmouth College in a commencement address in 2015. In it, he encouraged the graduates to make four commitments: (1) to spouse and to family, (2) to a career and a vocation, (3) to faith or philosophy, and (4) to a community and a village. These four commitments may be good to jot down in a journal somewhere and occasionally think about during your college years. How is college forming you for these commitments? In what ways are you better prepared to think about these areas? You may not be ready to make all these commitments by the time of your graduation ceremony, but you should have a foundation to consider these great commitments.

Commitment is an act of love. Commitment forms gritty people with a deep sense of purpose, meaning, and personhood. Hannah Arendt warns, "Without being bound to the fulfillment of our promises, we would never be able to keep our identities. We would be condemned to wander helplessly and without direction in the darkness of each person's lonely heart, caught in its contradictions and equivocalities."[6] You need to make commitments for a meaningful and purposeful life. The world needs the type of people who are willing to be vulnerable and to be hurt, but with the moral conviction and resolve to stay. The world needs people who can make commitments.

True knowledge of a subject makes us responsible. Knowledge asks you a question: what will you do with what you know? Lord willing, throughout your college career, you will ask and be asked that question over and over. What will you do with the knowledge you gained? How will you seek to apply it? What difference did these four years make? The more knowledge you have, the more responsible you become.

Setting You Back on the Pilgrim's Path

In the David Foster Wallace commencement address that I referenced, he mentions whole areas of mundane life that you know nothing about. He references things like going to the grocery store after a long week of work because you did not have time to do so earlier. All you want to do is go in and get out, but traffic, people, and the store layout make this difficult for you. Now, you have probably done something like this before, but it's not yet been a habit of your life. In those moments, your education will matter. Remember that your education is not about what you know but about how you pay attention—how you imagine the world.

In your college years, these mundane experiences could be on a random Tuesday at 1 pm after lunch in your junior year. And you'll think, "Why does this stupid math problem matter?" Or it could be an opportunity to go to a party, even though you're underage. "It's just once," you'll think.

Or it could be after college. I hate to break it to you, but you probably won't get your dream job right out of college. You may have an entry-level job that won't be as fulfilling as you'd hoped. There will be trials and boredom that pale in comparison to writing a paper.

The truth is that you are always becoming what you will become. You have a choice about how to worship in your daily deeds and tasks. Your commitments will reflect your love, which will govern how you respond in these moments. Your education and the habits you choose will form how you pay attention. You pay attention to what you love. You will be a certain type of person based on the decisions you make in mundane moments. Your pilgrimage in college sets you on a trajectory for your pilgrimage through life.

Benediction

Frederick Buechner once wrote, "The grace of God means something like this: 'Here is your life. You might never have been, but you are, because the party wouldn't have been the same without you. Here is the world. Beautiful and terrible things will happen. Don't be afraid. I am with you...I love you.'"[7]

So, pilgrim, you are on a journey. On this path, you will encounter the world. Your life in college is part of the pilgrimage. You are going somewhere pointed in a certain destination. Beautiful and terrible things will happen. But don't be afraid. The God of the universe is with you. He loves you.

Discussion Questions

1. What's difficult or scary about making commitments?
2. David Brooks says that college is about making four commitments: to a faith/philosophy, family/spouse, community/village, and career/vocation. Which commitments do you feel most prepared to make? Which commitments do you hope college will shape you to make?
3. At the end of this book, do you have a clearer idea about your identity and your purpose? How so?

Notes

1. Jonathan Franzen, "Liking is for Cowards: Go for What Hurts," *The New York Times*, May 28, 2011, https://www.nytimes.com/2011/05/29/opinion/29franzen.html.

2. GK Chesterton, *The Autobiography of GK Chesterton* (New York: Sheed and Ward, 1936), 288-89.

3. David Brooks, "The Ultimate Spoiler Alert," commencement address at Dartmouth University, Hanover, New Hampshire, June 14, 2015, https://news.dartmouth.edu/news/2015/06/david-brooks-commencement-address.

4. Parker Palmer, *To Know as We Are Known: A Spirituality of Education* (San Francisco: Harper & Row, 1983), 65.

5. Timothy Keller and Michael Keller, "University Missions and Evangelism Today" in *Serving the Church, Reaching the World: Essays in Honour of Don Carson,* ed. Richard Cunningham (London: Inter-Varsity, 2017).

6. Hannah Arendt, quoted in Gary Thomas, *The Sacred Marriage* (Grand Rapids: Zondervan, 2000), 11.

7. Frederick Buechner, *Wishful Thinking: A Seeker's ABC* (San Francisco: HarperOne, 1993), 39.

ACKNOWLEDGMENTS

I am not an impressive person. That's not false humility; it's a true reality. And it means I have a lot to acknowledge. One of my favorite verses in the Bible is a rhetorical question: what do you have that you have not received? (1 Cor. 4:7). Of course, the answer is nothing. I have nothing that has not been a gift. Another way to think about acknowledgment is to recognize the abundance of gifts and graces that God has given me.

My parents were both educators. My mom worked as an elementary school teacher, and my dad taught science and math in high school before teaching in the nuclear power industry. He also coached soccer, which is teaching of its own form. But I come from a heritage of teachers, I suppose, and I did not plan to take up the family lineage, but here I am. Two weeks ago, I met a man who was maybe late forties and early fifties who said, "Sosler? That's a unique name. I had a first-grade teacher named Mrs. Sosler." After a few subsequent questions, that first grade teacher from 40-plus years ago was my mom. He said she was one of the best teachers he ever had. When I'm with my dad, sometimes we run into his old students in the nuclear power plant. These former students regularly disclose what a good teacher and how helpful he was in their career. All this to say, this book is dedicated to them. I have never doubted their love for me, and now as a parent, that's about all I hope my kids can say about me as a father. Their love has taught me a lot.

In relation to this book, there are a few specific acknowledgments. I'm in higher education because the kindness of a few colleagues. My first academic conference was at Baylor University in Waco, Texas. I found out one of my college friends, Sam, (now godfather of my firstborn son) was going with his dad. I presented and those folks said nice things, but people say nice things. I'm cynical and didn't think much of it. A few weeks later, Sam's dad emailed me about a job that he was passing my resume on to. This felt different. It's one thing to say something nice; it's another to do something nice and put your name behind it. Sam's dad is David Guthrie who wrote the Foreword. I can't thank him enough for his support and wisdom through the years. When you love, you give.

A few years later, I went back to that conference at Baylor with the same professors I met with Sam. While there, they suggested I start writing. I never thought about that, because I never really had the confidence that anyone would care what I thought. One of those encouragers is named Keith Martel. He runs Falls City Press and has been a consistent source of nurture and refinement throughout this writing process, and a joy to work with.

A few housekeeping acknowledgments. The conceptual scheme of the first half of this book and the four ages of the university started in my dissertation under John David Trentham. I thank him for his patient guidance and wisdom throughout the process. A condensed but more academic argument can also be found in the academic journal *Christian Higher Education.*[1] An extended argument of a sacramental vision in education versus a worldview approach found in Chapter 7 can be found in *Christian Scholars Review.*[2] The genesis of Chapter 8 was in *Pro Rege* journal in an issue commemorating the 500th anniversary of Dordt.[3] All of these publications have sharpened my arguments in this book.

Lastly, to Lauren and my kids: Mariela, Auden, and Jude. While my parents nurtured me into physical life, you have taught me what it means to truly live. I thought I knew what love was before I met you, but marriage and parenting has been a school of love. The classroom made me understand who I was and am in relationship to the world. You all have taught me to love that world I find myself in, because the world has been sweeter and richer by knowing and loving you in it. You are the world's best gifts. And I don't "acknowledge" that enough.

Notes

1. Alex Sosler, "Typology of Higher Education: Analyzing the Purposes of Learning" *Christian Higher Education* (2022) 22.4.

2. Alex Sosler, "Going to School with Marilynne Robinson: Sacramental Education as Alternative Paradigm for Faith Integration" *Christian Scholars Review* (Fall 2022) LI:4.

3.Alex Sosler, "Prodigal Love and a Hermeneutic of Charity: How Grace Changes Learning" *Pro Rege* (March 18, 2020) 48.3: 23-28.

ABOUT THE AUTHOR

Alex Sosler is assistant professor of Bible and Ministry at Montreat College. Prior to higher education, he served in ministry in his hometown of Cleveland, Ohio, as well as Austin, Texas. He is currently an Assisting Priest at Redeemer Anglican Church in Asheville, North Carolina.

Alex's research focuses on theology and the arts, spiritual formation, and education. His popular writing has been featured on the *Front Porch Republic*, *Mockingbird*, *Fathom Magazine*, *Christ and Pop Culture*, *FareForward*, *Church Life Journal*, and *Gospel-Centered Discipleship*.

Alex resides in Asheville with his wife, Lauren, and their three children, Mariela, Auden, and Jude.

www.alexsosler.com

OTHER WORKS BY ALEX SOSLER

Wholeness and Holiness: Truth, Goodness, Beauty,
and Community for the Life of the Soul
Baker Academic
(Spring 2024)

Sacramental Imagination: Connecting Spiritual Vision
and Artistic Practice
Co-written With Gary Ball
Cascade Books
(Fall 2024)

Edited Volume

Theology and the Avett Brothers
Foreword by James KA Smith
Afterword by Bob Crawford
Lexington Books/Fortress Academic

Made in the USA
Columbia, SC
20 November 2023

26474376R00138